Saint Bonaventure

EFREM BETTONI

Translated by

ANGELUS GAMBATESE, O.F.M.

UNIVERSITY OF NOTRE DAME PRESS • 1964

Originally published in Italian by
"La Scuola," Editrice, Brescia, Italy, as

S. BONAVENTURA

Copyright © 1964 by the
University of Notre Dame Press
Notre Dame, Indiana

Library of Congress Catalog Card Number: 64-22164

Manufactured in the United States

CONTENTS

I

The Historical and
Spiritual Figure of

SAINT BONAVENTURE

HIS LIFE

St. Bonaventure has suffered the same fate as all the great thinkers of the thirteenth century: they have found many admirers and students of their works, but no devoted compiler of their memoirs, no one who would attempt a living spiritual profile which would have helped posterity to penetrate into the depth of their souls with the help of facts other than those which can be culled from their writings. This can be explained in terms of the spirit of the great century so impassioned for ideas and so disinterested in concrete facts. And yet St. Bonaventure profoundly impressed his contemporaries not only with the depth of his thought and the coherence of his doctrine, but also with his administrative accomplishments.

The available historical data regarding him concern mostly his external activity. Information on things and events bearing on his inward life are scarce, extremely brief, fragmentary and uncertain. The first life of St. Bonaventure was not written until near the end of the fifteenth century by Mariano of Florence, almost 200 years after his death. I shall not include in this short biographical survey all the historical information which pertains to St. Bonaventure,[1] but only that which will shed light on the spiritual aspect of his life and activity.

[1] The more modern and complete studies on the life of St. Bonaventure are: *Vita seraphici Doctoris per*

3

The Seraphic Doctor was born in the little town of Bagnorea (today called Cività di Bagnorea) near Viterbo, in either 1221 or 1222. The uncertainty as to the time of his birth is explained by the fact that all we know historically is that he died in 1274 at the age of 53. Mariano of Florence tells us that his father was a doctor and his name was John "of the noble house of Fedenza," while his mother's name was Ritella.

St. Bonaventure's Franciscan vocation had an early origin. As a child he was miraculously cured by St. Francis. "My mother having prayed to blessed Father Francis for me when I was gravely ill as a child," he writes in the *Legenda minor*,[2] "I was delivered by him from the jaws of death and restored to a healthy life." This historical nucleus has undergone legendary embellishment. St. Francis on this occasion is supposed to have exclaimed "O buona ventura," thus giving a new name to the predestined child. It is almost certain, however, that the cure occurred after the Poverello had died.

Along with this cause for gratitude can be added— besides the interior action of grace—the reflections

---

     modum annalium enarrata, Opera Omnia S. Bonaventurae (Ad Claras Aquas: Collegium S. Bonaventurae, 1882-1891), t. X, pp. 39-73; Leonard Lemmens, *Der hl. Bonaventura, Kardinal und Kirchenlehrer aus dem Franziskanerorden;* also the first chapter of Etienne Gilson's *La Philosophie de S. Bonaventure* (Paris: J. Vrin, 1924).

[2] "Voto pro me languente gravissime ad beatum Patrem Franciscum emisso a matre, cum adhuc essem puerulus, ab ipso sum portis faucibus erutus et in robur vitae incolumis restitutus." *Legenda minor S. Francisci; Omnia Opera,* t. VIII, p. 579.

which St. Bonaventure made on the marvelous development of the Franciscan Order. "I confess before God, that He made me especially love the life of blessed Francis because it is like the beginning and perfection of the Church, which first began from simple fishermen and afterward included expert and renowned doctors; so you will see the same thing in the Order of blessed Francis, that God might give evidence that it was not founded through the prudence of men but through Christ. And because the works of Christ do not fail but progress, it is thus shown that this work was divine, since even learned men did not disdain to join the companionship of the simple."[3] This same scientific development within the Franciscan Order had made Blessed Giles exclaim: "Paris, Paris, you have destroyed Assisi," and Jacopone to lament,

> Tal'è, qual'è, tal'è,
> Non c'è religione
> Mal vedemmo Parisi
> Ch' n'ha destrutto Assisi
> Con la lor lettoria
> L'han messo in mala via.

[3] "Fateor coram Deo, quod me fecit vitam beati Francisci maxime diligere, quia similis est initio et perfectioni Ecclesiae, quae primo incepit a piscatoribus simplicibus et postmodum profecit ad doctores clarissimos et peritissimos: sic videbis in Religione beati Francisci, ut ostendat Deus, quod non fuit per hominum prudentiam inventa, sed per Christum: et quia opera Christi non deficiunt, sed proficiunt, ostenditur, hoc opus fuisse divinum, dum ad consortium virorum simplicium etiam sapientes non sunt dedignati descendere." *Epistola de tribus quaestionibus*, n. 13; *Omnia Opera*, t. VIII, p. 336.

It is regarded by St. Bonaventure, on the other hand, as the divine seal of approval on the institution of St. Francis.

But where was young Bonaventure at the time which gave him the opportunity to admire this remarkable spread of the Order which decided him on the Franciscan vocation? The place most apt to suggest such reflections was Paris where celebrated Franciscan doctors lived and taught. There was John de la Rochelle, Odo Rigaldi, William of Melitona, and especially Alexander of Hales, the greatest of them all, who, already an old and esteemed master, had entered the Order of the Poverello of Assisi in 1231. In so doing, Alexander created quite a sensation at the time.

The young Fedenza must then have gone to study at Paris before joining the friars, and there at the school of Alexander his Franciscan vocation matured. This is one more reason which causes me to place the date of his entrance into the Order in the year 1243, rather than 1238, the year in which he probably went to Paris to study and became the disciple of Alexander who, as was then the custom, taught at the Franciscan friary there.

The University of Paris was not organized as are the universities of today which have their seat in specific buildings. The mediaeval university was merely a corporation of masters and students with its own laws and statutes. The master located his school wherever he wished, and at their own convenience the students went to the lectures of the master whom they preferred. The solemn academic functions were usually held in some hall of the episcopal residence.

The scholarly career of St. Bonaventure was rapid

and had developed almost parallel to that of St. Thomas. In 1248, as a Bachelor of Arts—a title which corresponds more or less to the modern university instructor—he began to explain Sacred Scripture, which was followed in 1250-1251 by an exposition of the Sentences of Peter Lombard. In 1253-1254 he received his licentiate. One more step, however, still remained before he could reach the top of the academic hierarchy: his proclamation as Master. There was to be much opposition before its final announcement.

In protest against maltreatment of some of the university students by the police during a brawl, all the masters of the university went on strike and suspended their lectures.[4] Only the Dominican and Franciscan masters continued to teach. The other masters resented this lack of solidarity and decreed that from that time on no one would be given the title of master unless he had taken an oath to observe all the statutes of the university. The controversy was referred to the Pope. Innocent IV, and after him Alexander IV, intervened vigorously in favor of the mendicants. But while things seemed smooth again, the situation became more threatening.

Defeated in the quarrel regarding the statutes of the university, which resulted in their being modified by Alexander IV in his bull *Quasi lignum vitae* (April

---

[4] This was not the first time that the University of Paris had recourse to a strike to obtain justice. In identical circumstances a student strike had been called in 1229, and Pope Gregory IX, who had intervened to settle the controversy, conceded to the members of the university the right of recourse if they could not obtain the justice due to them.

14, 1255), the masters, with William of Saint Amour
as their spokesman, contested not only the mendicants' right to teach, but also their very right to
exist. In the book *De periculis novissimorum tempo-
rum,* their way of life was declared impossible and
described as dangerous to the Church. Only the energetic intervention of the Pope succeeded in first re-
straining and then quelling the tempest which had
its source in twisted human emotions. St. Thomas
and St. Bonaventure fought side by side during the
controversy and confirmed the victory of their Orders
when they both received the doctoral degree October
23, 1257.[5]

The Angelic Doctor, however advanced with all
his tremendous energy in the academic field of speculation, while the Seraphic Doctor, in the same year
that he became a doctor at Paris, was elected Minister
General of the Franciscan Order, at the age of thirty-
six. Instead of finding the serenity of intellectual research, he was immersed in the administrative task of
ruling an Order now spread over all of Europe and
already beginning the conquest of Asia with heroic
missionary endeavors. At the same time the Order
was undergoing a period of crisis. St. Bonaventure's
predecessor, Blessed John of Parma, had steadfastly
refused to be re-elected General by the Chapter precisely because he had despaired of settling the internal
situation of the Order, which was divided into three
factions, and most difficult to reconcile.

[5] The friendship between the two holy Doctors is
   historically certain, although the episodes described
   by later historians who attempt to put this friendship
   in relief are not as certain. Cf. Lemmens, *op. cit.,*
   pp. 85 and 267.

St. Francis had conceived his Order as a fraternity of men who pledged themselves to observe to the letter the poverty of the Holy Gospel. Rather than have so-called convents, they were to have meeting places—for the most part near a church and in solitary places—where together they would give themselves to prayer and penance, each one according to his inspiration. The Rule was the Gospel and the heroic love of each for Jesus Christ. We can understand that St. Francis did not feel the necessity of external organization, but we can also understand that in the face of human reality this ideal in its purity became impossible to follow for a great many men. The advice of Cardinal Ugolino finally induced St. Francis to write the definitive Rule of 1223 which, if it did not establish the complete organization of the Order, at least did not preclude its possibility.

Every human organization must have its feet well planted on the ground and must be concretized in exterior institutions. The Franciscan life, no longer abandoned to the inspiration of the individual, demanded the community life and the permanence of the convent. Furthermore, the apostolic life decreed by St. Francis for his friars demanded suitable intellectual preparation, because it was not possible for heroic sanctity to substitute for learning in everyone as in the Poverello and his first companions. Thus there was need of buildings and for a suitable environment. While human logic urged the development of the Order in this direction, the Church also fostered it for she saw in the Order a formidable force for the Christian renewal of society.

One can also understand that the witnesses of the early days of the Order and those who were living in the light of the ideal of the Holy Founder became increasingly aloof and had difficulty seeing the necessity of many innovations especially since in many friars there was a pronounced tendency to go to extremes in this matter of innovations, thus placing the very originality of the Order in jeopardy. The majority of the Franciscans, however, favored a middle solution: absolute fidelity to the substance of the Franciscan ideal and complete acceptance of the pontifical declarations on the Rule of 1223. On this path St. Bonaventure resolutely placed himself, and during his eighteen years of wise and enlightened rule he dedicated his best efforts to the task of achieving this balance in the whole Order. That he was prepared for this undertaking was due not only to the innate equilibrium of his nature, but also to the fact that his vocation had matured and his Franciscan formation had been accomplished in the atmosphere of Paris. "It was the happy disposition of divine Providence," writes Father Lemmens,[6] "that Bonaventure

[6] Lemmens, *op. cit.,* p. 42.

entered religious life at Paris. If he had passed his first years in a small convent in Italy and in the restricted environment of many friars of that time, it would have been most difficult for him to acquire such broad vision and his own personal conception of the Franciscan ideal, which he was to manifest later on during his generalate and which made him the second founder of the Order."

The line of conduct which he followed in governing the Order was this: respect and admiration for those friars who, enlightened by divine inspiration, wished to live the primitive Franciscan ideal in all its purity; inflexible rigor with all who sought to stretch the Rule and Franciscan poverty beyond the legitimate pontifical interpretations; energetic effort to lead the Order back to the full observance of the Rule of 1223. He hoped to achieve the proper balance with which to solve all of its difficulties. St. Bonaventure contributed to this restoration not only by the wisdom of his legislation and the prestige of his sanctity, but also by the doctrine of his writings with which he enlightened minds and justified his conduct.

History tells us that the generous effort of St. Bonaventure failed. After his death the Order plunged into an even more serious crisis. The Spirituals (the historical name of the intransigent Franciscans), inspired in their struggle for poverty by the alleged visions of Abbot Joachim of Flora, again upset the Order, fell into heresy and threatened to ruin the work of St. Francis. But these exaggerations only served to place in relief the wisdom of the way chosen by St. Bonaventure and, as a result, his way became the guide for all future reformers of the Franciscan Order.

His work was highly valued by the Supreme Pontiffs, who many times sought to persuade him to assume the direction of important dioceses. He succeeded, however, in avoiding them until finally Gregory X, in June 1273, named him Cardinal-Bishop of Albano with the categorical injunction of accepting it. Bonaventure bowed to obedience and hastened to join the Papal court near Florence. Mariano of Florence relates that when the papal legates arrived at the convent to give him the Cardinal's hat, the Minister General was busy washing the dishes. Gregory's choice was not merely a recognition of Bonaventure's learning and activity; the Pope desired to have him completely at the service of the Church, especially on the occasion of the council to be convoked at Lyons in May 1274. At a General Chapter of the Order which he called in the same city Bonaventure resigned his office as Minister General.

He was now free to dedicate all his efforts to the work of the council and he played a major role in the reunion of the Greeks with Rome, a union already prepared for by the Franciscans he had sent to the Orient. The reunion came about with great solemnity and jubilation on July 6, 1274. But partly because of the extraordinary fatigue resulting from the council and partly, perhaps, because of the great joy from the religious peace reattained, the weakened constitution of Bonaventure gave out completely.

The Seraphic Doctor died early Sunday morning, July 15, 1274, only eight days after the historical union of the Greeks with Rome. The Fathers of the Lyons Council, both Latin and Greek, with the Pope and the whole Pontifical Curia assisted at his funeral, which was one of the most solemn that the history of the Church has recorded.

ST. BONAVENTURE AND THE PROBLEMS OF HIS TIME

Typical of all the thirteenth-century masters, St. Bonaventure was called upon to pass judgment on Aristotle. It is clear to all familiar with the Middle Ages that the tremendous speculative dynamism of that century neither was nor could be simply a lively dialectical skirmish. It was a welter of profound and concrete contrasts which arose from the very complexity of the great philosophical problems.

In the thirteenth century the great philosophical traditions—Greek, Christian and Arabic—met for the first time. Plato, Aristotle, Plotinus, Augustine, Avicenna and Averroes—even if not always with their genuine works—mixed their powerful and discordant voices in the schools, where great intellects sought a synthesis of them all in the harmony of the Christian faith. If "the heavens manifest the glory of God" (Psalm 18, verse 1), why could not these giants of thought compose a harmonious hymn to the highest Truth?

The new and more powerful voice was that of Aristotle and the tremendous importance of this philosopher could not fail to command the attention of St. Thomas Aquinas who, in his capacity as master at the University of Paris, strove for this intellectual synthesis. In the years which followed, Aquinas—having studied the thought of Aristotle in the commen-

taries of St. Albert the Great and the translations of
his confrère William of Moerbeke—devoted himself
to the re-elaboration of all Christian thought according to the spirit and method of the new philosophy
and defended tenaciously the legitimacy of his stand
against the Averroists and the Augustinians. During
this time St. Bonaventure was absorbed in the cares
of the Order, the responsibility of which, as Minister
General, he carried before the Church and the world.

He was not, however, disinterested in the new intellectual developments which were coming about at
the University of Paris. Normally he lived in this city
and left it only when the care of the friars and the
affairs of the Order demanded it. Many things kept
him at Paris: the importance which the university
had assumed in the intellectual life of Europe, for it
had become the greatest center of Catholic thought;
the curiosity of the born thinker who could not be
a stranger to intellectual problems; the memories
of his religious and academic life spent there; the
opportuneness and efficacy of his presence and of his
teaching in that convent where the best young men
of all the provinces of the Order came in large num-
bers. Nor should it be forgotten that John Peckham
who, in opposition to St. Thomas, was the most
ardent defender of the genuine Augustinian tradition,
had been a disciple of St. Bonaventure. One can
easily understand that the Seraphic Doctor had full
knowledge of the noble experiment undertaken by
his holy friend Thomas.

Nevertheless, he did not adopt Thomas' synthesis
but continued in his former line of thought, per-
fecting as much as time would allow his own synthesis of Augustinian philosophy already well delineated

in his *Commentary on the Sentences of Peter Lombard*—the result of his teaching at Paris in the years 1250-1257. Later I will have occasion to speak of what Bonaventure thought of Aristotle and his philosophy, but at this time it seems proper to discuss a question which spontaneously presents itself to our mind: what were the motives which led the Seraphic Doctor to prefer the path which passes through Plato and Augustine to that which passes through Aristotle?

Certainly his formation as a youth in the school of Alexander of Hales was an important factor. It is difficult to free one's self from the intellectual point of departure from which the mind began its journey toward truth and which teachers—especially when truly worthy of this title—expounded with fervent conviction. But it is also evident that this reason is an insufficient answer to our question. It would be equivalent to reducing St. Bonaventure to the stature of a philosopher without intellectual power and originality. A thinker who has not measured with his own eyes all the possible ways of arriving at the truth, and has not made a choice based on reasons acquired and evaluated by himself, is not worthy of the name of philosopher. Furthermore, it is quite probable that while he was at Paris Bonaventure also followed the lectures of St. Albert the Great, at least for a time.[1]

Men of such undisputed authority as the editors of the *Opera Omnia* of St. Bonaventure express the opinion that he did not follow the Angelic Doctor in his Christian Neo-Aristotelianism because the affairs

---

[1] Leonard Lemmens, *Der hl. Bonaventura, Kardinal und Kirchenlehrer aus dem Franziskanerorden*, p. 46.

of the Order prevented him from becoming acquainted with Aristotle through the new translations, and hence it was impossible for him to appreciate the importance and richness of Aristotle's thought. "He had already begun to teach and write his principal work, the *Commentary on the Sentences,* while still a young man, before that new system of studies (the Aristotelianism of St. Thomas) appeared. However, in a short time he had to renounce his academic studies and lectures in order to assume the rule of a great Order while scarcely 34 years of age. Whence he could not fully develop the potentialities of his genius and doctrine as St. Thomas was able to do."[2] Father Lemmens agrees with this appraisal: ". . . Thomas was the first among the great Christian thinkers to find himself in the happy condition of knowing the true and genuine Stagirite. Because of the acuteness of his ingenuity he knew enough to profit from this circumstance, thus opening the way to a new period of Christian philosophy. Bonaventure, on the other hand, was not in the position to profit by this progress, and this is the principal reason for the difference which is found on certain points between his doctrine and that of his friend Thomas."[3]

This opinion supposes two things: first, that all persons of genius, and therefore St. Bonaventure also, must necessarily embrace Aristotelianism if they have the opportunity of reaching the full maturity of their thought; second, that St. Thomas and St. Bonaventure follow essentially the same path and diverge only on certain points. Today few scholars are disposed

[2] *Opera Omnia,* t. X, p. 31.
[3] Lemmens, *op. cit.,* p. 70.

to subscribe to this opinion without qualification. The answer which is commonly given at the present time to the question which we have proposed is a different one and it must be sought in the fidelity of St. Bonaventure to the Franciscan ideal.

The easiest way to discover in its integrity the spirit which pervades the formulas of a philosophical system, which unifies and enlivens them, is to find the central problem that this system proposes to resolve. What, then, is the problem which St. Bonaventure pondered? What is the experience he wished to explain in his works?

The problem for which St. Bonaventure sought a solution was that of St. Francis of Assisi. The thing which struck his contemporaries the most in St. Francis was his poverty, that absolute despoilment of all the things of this world which he had placed at the foundation of his religious life. St. Bonaventure, however, was not satisfied with this merely negative aspect. Evidently Franciscan poverty has no value in itself; it is a means of arriving at that perfect union with God which one admires so much in St. Francis. His life was transformed into a kind of continual contact with God—a contact which was realized not only in solitude, in prayer or at the time of ecstasy, but also in his simple daily living. Things seen through the spiritualized eyes of the Poverello testify to the divine perfections and divine love calling us back to spiritual realities. For him the world was an immense forest of symbols which redirect the mind and heart to God. In this fashion the Franciscan "contempt of the world" is reconciled with that sympathy which communes with all creation. Things in themselves are nothing, but they have value and are lovable because of what they signify.

The fundamental significance and teaching of the Franciscan life is precisely this: to recall men to this continual contemplation of God which is the knowledge and the peace to which every man must aspire, for it is the very purpose of his existence. This is what St. Bonaventure wished to save of the Franciscan ideal at all cost. This is the essential aspect of it and the particular manner of accomplishing this goal is of little importance.

At this point the Seraphic Doctor adds something to the teachings and the practices of St. Francis. The Poverello saw in study and in the love for knowledge a serious obstacle for anyone who wished to follow him in his detachment from the world and his flight toward heaven. He who studies desires to possess books, easily becomes attached to learning and puffed up by his knowledge. Characteristic of this attitude are the episodes narrated in the first chapter of *The Mirror of Perfection* which, even if not the work of Brother Leo, reflect the sentiments of the first generation of Franciscans.

"The measure of a man's knowledge," St. Francis said to one who had asked permission to acquire books, "is according to his works, and the religious is a good speaker inasmuch as his works are good." And on another occasion: "There are so many who willingly acquire knowledge, that those are blessed who remain ignorant for the love of the Lord God." Thus it seemed to the Spirituals that the flowering of studies in the Order was a betrayal of the Franciscan ideal, and that the voice of Paris was extinguishing the divine teaching of Assisi.

St. Bonaventure clearly understood that the ignorant and illiterate could arrive, as did St. Francis, at the highest contemplation, for it is above all the work of grace and prayer. At the same time, however, he affirms just as unequivocally that besides the way of ascetic heroism, not possible to all, there is the discipline of the intellect. The work of the thinker must be an "itinerarium mentis," that is, an intellectual striving toward the peace of contemplation: a theory and, at the same time, a way of life that justified before all his confrères the support which he gave to study, without betraying in the least the substance of the ideal of St. Francis of Assisi.

It is not difficult now to explain the proper character of Bonaventurian speculation: its intimate essential religious quality; its constant rapport with theology in relation to which it is but an admirable meditation; its mysticism, which determines both the point of arrival and the method which is based more on the rhythm of analogy than on rigorous logical sequence; that affective warmth through which every step is at the same time an act of understanding and an act of love. Nor is it difficult to explain why St. Bonaventure preferred St. Augustine and Christian Neo-Platonism to the new Aristotelian philosophy. The method of Platonic-Augustinian thought is indeed a study or a vision of reality which takes its point of departure from unity, while the Aristotelian method is essentially a movement from multiplicity to unity. The former—and the whole history of philosophy gives evidence of this—tends to place in relief the dependence of things on God and the immanence of the divine in the creature. The latter accents the independent existence of things, the value which they have in themselves. The Platonist sees things in God; the Aristotelian sees God at the summit of things. If both philosophies lead to religion, it is undeniable that the religious element is more spontaneous in a philosophy of the Platonic type for it penetrates its very structure. In order to confirm the truth of what I have been saying, one needs only to open any of the works of St. Bonaventure.

His choice, then, is more than justified by the fact that he reflected not in order to know God but in order to love Him; in order to carry out, as much as possible on this earth, that which will be the eternal inheritance of man in heaven.

HIS WORKS

In the *Opera Omnia* of St. Bonaventure we read the following statement of the editors: ". . . in the past centuries, as many have observed, the excellent doctrine of St. Bonaventure, although always verbally praised, lay for the most part neglected and almost forgotten, except for a few men who really understood it."[1] We can very well change the past tense of the verbs in this quotation to the present, for these words still apply today. And this notwithstanding the fact that the above-mentioned editors have placed at the disposal of all a critical edition of the works of the Seraphic Doctor, which still remains a model unsurpassed in its field.

It must be acknowledged that the reading of St. Bonaventure's works is difficult for those who have not been introduced to his thought and method, and this for two reasons. The first is the extraordinarily synthetic character of his system and his expositive method, on account of which every page is so interrelated with the whole that it becomes comprehensible only to him who knows the whole system. If this is true of every philosopher, it is particularly true of St. Bonaventure.

The second reason for the difficult reading is that the Seraphic Doctor is the most mediaeval thinker of

---

[1] *Opera Omnia*, General Preface, p. ii.

all the masters of the thirteenth century—if "mediaeval thinker" means one who sees and perceives in a religious context all the manifestations and forms of reality and life. This places him, more than the others, far from our modern sensibility with its conspicuously naturalistic flavor.

The penetration of St. Bonaventure's thought, however, which results only from a constant reading of his texts, is an experience somewhat akin to that of St. Augustine while he perused the pages of Sacred Scripture, and it will verify in all of Bonaventure's works what Gerson said of the *Breviloquium* and the *Itinerarium Mentis in Deum*: "For more than thirty years I have striven to familiarize myself with them, pondering them continuously word by word. For all that, in all this time I have scarcely succeeded in tasting them. As often as I read them they always seem to afford me new delights."[2]

The writings of St. Bonaventure can be divided into five groups. The first contains his doctrinal works which are theoretical in character; second, his exegetical works; third, his mystical and ascetical works; fourth, all his writings which in some manner pertain to the religious life and especially Franciscanism; and fifth, all his sermons.

It is not necessary for our purposes to give a complete enumeration of all the works of the Seraphic Doctor. It will be more useful to give a brief explanation of those writings which have special importance for the understanding of his philosophical thought. As for the rest, I will mention only the most im-

---

[2] Leonard Lemmens, *Der hl. Bonaventura, Kardinal und Kirchenlehrer aus dem Franziskanerorden*, p. 73.

portant or those which are available either in separate editions or in translation.

1. *Commentaria in quatuor libros sententiarum Magistri Petri Lombardi*

This is the most important work for the understanding of St. Bonaventure's philosophical thought. It takes up the first four tomes of the Quaracchi edition. Almost all of the great mediaeval masters, from Alexander of Hales on, have written a *Commentary on the Sentences of Peter Lombard* which is always divided into four books. This commentary was compiled during the master's years at the university, and is merely a definitive editing of the lectures held by the author as a Bachelor of Arts. Usually it is a work of one's early years in which the mind of the young professor undertakes a philosophical and theological synthesis for the first time. While in the case of St. Thomas his *Commentary on the Sentences* is surpassed by his two *Summae,* for St. Bonaventure it remains the principal source for the understanding of his thought. He has written, it is true, other works which, as we shall see, are of primary importance. But because of their extremely synthetic character they cannot take the place of a perusal and study of the great *Commentary.* These minor works, all found in Tome V of the Quaracchi edition, are the following:

2. *Quaestiones disputatae de scientia Christi, de mysterio Trinitatis, de perfectione evangelica*

The title may be misleading. Although it treats of theological problems, this work also includes excellent philosophical passages on divine knowledge, intellectual illumination, and the existence and attributes of God. Pages are dedicated to these subjects, and they are dealt with more analytically and with more precision than in the *Commentary on the Sentences*.

3. *Breviloquium*

More than the others, this work affords us the opportunity of seeing the concrete application of the Bonaventurian method. It is a brief *summa* of dogmatic theology which is divided into seven parts. The first two especially, entitled "De Trinitate Dei" and "De creatura mundi," offer us a precious synthesis of Bonaventurian theodicy, cosmology and psychology.

4. *Itinerarium mentis in Deum*

While this is the most famous work of St. Bonaventure, a true understanding of its content is not as easy to achieve as its popularity would indicate. Furthermore, this little work is not of purely philosophical value. It was written to teach the soul to contemplate God in all creatures: material, spiritual, and above all in the human soul enriched by the gifts of nature and grace. It is a true meditation, in the religious sense of the word, and hence is imbued with prayer and guided by the loving anxiety of the soul which yearns for the supreme peace of rapture in God. It is, however, the meditation of a metaphysician and a theologian which is developed on the level of concepts finely spun from his own thought, to which philosophy and theology offer all their fruits. Another important point to keep in mind is that the *Itinerarium* is not a demonstration of the existence of God. It is a way marked out for enlightened and desirous minds by which they might arrive at the most perfect possible union with God through knowledge. It indicates the essentially religious nature of all intellectual activity, which for St. Bonaventure constituted the only justification for speculation.

5. *Opusculum de reductione artium ad theologiam*

This treatise, while small in content, is an indispensable introduction for the understanding of St. Bonaventure's works, especially the *Itinerarium*. It contains the theory of what we see in the *Itinerarium* in practice. All human knowledge mirrors in its contents the threefold teaching of Sacred Scripture: the eternal generation and the Incarnation of Christ; the right order of living; and the union of the soul with God. And this teaching is more profound and more substantial than all purely human knowledge. To engage in the latter without reference to the former is to condemn one's activity to impoverishment and sterility. The method of Bonaventurian thought leads by its very nature to the discovery of God.

6. *Collationes in Hexaemeron*

This work, which remains unfinished because of Bonaventure's elevation to the Cardinalate, contains the conferences held at the University of Paris, the purpose of which was to warn the members of the university of the errors which were making headway everywhere and especially within their ranks. Substantially, these conferences were in opposition to the Aristotelian naturalism which was producing such bitter fruit in the Averroistic atmosphere. This point alone is sufficient to indicate the great philosophical importance of these conferences: they reveal to us the basic motives on which the anti-Aristotelianism of St. Bonaventure rests.

7. *Collationes de septem donis Spiritus Sancti*
8. *Collationes de decem praeceptis*
9. *Sermones selecti de rebus theologicis*

These three treatises, and particularly the last, must
not be forgotten by anyone who wishes to get a complete grasp even of only the philosophy of St. Bonaventure.

Among the other works of St. Bonaventure, which
take up the remaining four large tomes of the Quaracchi edition—of more interest to the exegete, the
mystic or the Franciscan—I single out only the ten
shorter mystical works (*Decem opuscula ad theologiam mysticam in spectantia*) which form a substantial book of meditation for one who is already
familiar with Bonaventurian thought. I merely list
the titles here: *De triplici via (alias incendium
amoris), Soliloquium de IV mentalibus exercitiis,
Lignum vitae, De quinque festivitatibus pueri Jesus,
Tractatus de praeparatione ad missam, De perfectione vitae ad sorores, De regimine animae, De sex
alis seraphim, Officium de passione Domini,* and *Vitis
mystica.*

Among the writings particularly Franciscan, there
are the two on the life and miracles of St. Francis,
found in tome VIII of the *Opera Omnia* and entitled
Legenda maior S. Francisci and *Legenda minor S.
Francisci.*

There are fifty-five works of St. Bonaventure as-
sembled in the edition of Quaracchi, of which forty-
six are certainly authentic and nine are doubtful.

II

The Thought of

SAINT BONAVENTURE

KNOWLEDGE AND WISDOM

Every mediaeval thinker, theologian, or philosopher admitted without hesitation that there are two sources of human knowledge: revelation and reason. From the first proceed the truths of faith which have their foundation in the authority of God and the Church; from the second, natural truths founded on evidence. Spontaneously there arose the problem of determining the rapport and the competence of these two different modes of knowing. For every now and then the results of science, particularly philosophy, appeared to be in evident disagreement with that which must be held by faith. Was it necessary to explain the data of faith by placing it in accord with reason, or was it not necessary, on the other hand, to silence reason and accept only the voice of faith? In both alternatives the problem is resolved only with the suppression of one of the two terms: in the first, faith is reduced to reason; in the second the value of reason is denied in order to exalt faith.

There is a third solution, however, which resolves these two extreme answers to the problem. The truths of faith and the truths of reason have their source—the first directly, the second indirectly—in God; there cannot be, therefore, any real contradiction between the two. In the case of an apparent contradiction, one merely has to search out with good will the error which he has committed either in his interpretation of revelation or in his rational analysis. The contradiction is never objective; it is always subjective. It is never in reality; it is always in our thinking. This does not, however, resolve the problem in all its aspects.

Having acknowledged the respective value and method of faith and reason, a further question can be asked: Why is revelation necessary? Cannot reason alone solve all human problems and thus achieve its final end without recourse to revelation? This last question, in turn, can be treated either in the abstract or in the concrete. Considered in the abstract, the answer must be in the affirmative. For any other would be to admit that human nature is intrinsically imperfect and, therefore, incapable of attaining the complete development which is suitable to it. Man, then, must be capable of knowing all that is ordered to his perfection. But what precisely is the object to which the human intellect is ordered? Is it the totality of truth or only truth with certain limitations?

For St. Thomas the proper direct object of the human intellect is not reality as such but the quiddity of material things, "quidditas rei materialis," and only indirectly, that is, by inference, the spiritual reality which is God. Hence, although admitting the validity and sufficiency of reason in order that man might encompass all reality directly, an elevation is necessary on the part of God—an elevation which is begun here below with revelation and completed in eternity with the light of glory, the "lumen gloriae." Furthermore, because of the circumstances in which man finds himself in this life, circumstances which render his pursuit of truth long and arduous, revelation is *morally* necessary in order to give all men, and not just a few, the means of knowing the purpose of their life—and this easily, and in time to be useful. In the abstract, at least, the autonomy of reason and the possibility of a perfect philosophy is verified, namely, the possibility of a complete knowledge of all truth—always, however, within the limits proper to human reason.

St. Bonaventure has a different conception of the human intellect. Human understanding is made to know God as its final object, and the search for truth is the search for God. All knowledge is merely a step toward this goal. The material object of the human intellect is not changed with man's elevation to the supernatural order; the only change is in the perfection and manner by which the material object is attained. In other words, only the formal object is changed.

For St. Thomas, even in the integrity of his nature and with the full use of his energy, man could know God only through inference, through the process of reasoning, insofar as God is the cause and explanation of the world. In other words, man can know God naturally only by means of concepts. St. Bonaventure, as logical as the Angelic Doctor, having admitted that God is the proper and direct object of the human intellect, must concede to man, at least in the abstract, the possibility of a knowledge of God which is more perfect than conceptual knowledge, namely knowledge by way of inference, which is always indirect. St. Bonaventure calls this more perfect knowledge of God contemplation.[1] It is a

---

[1] Besides the "eye of the flesh" and the "eye of reason," St. Bonaventure also attributes to man the

knowledge of God indescribable for him who has not experienced it, of which one can only say that in this state the human mind no longer understands by means of concepts. It is a penetrating knowledge, inflamed with love; an act in which the greatest energies of the intellect and will blend together. It is not, however, that intuition of God reserved for glory which is not due to man and to which he arrives only because it has pleased God to raise him to the supernatural order. Up to this point we have been speaking in the abstract. In the concrete—in the actual condition of man—he easily strays from the path which leads to truth, and even if he should hit upon it he does not succeed in following it in all its developments.

For St. Bonaventure, then, an autonomous philosophical knowledge does not exist even in the abstract. If the goal of human knowledge is contemplation, philosophy or the activity of reason can only be a preparation, an initial step toward this goal. Much less, then, is such a knowledge possible in the concrete, given the distractions, the limitation and the obscurity within which the human mind moves— to which the history of philosophy gives ample testimony.

Reality is not a scattered manifold but a structured multiplicity bound together by an organic and wise plan which is manifested through many signs. This purpose, however, is not immediately acces-

---

"eye of contemplation": "Propter quam triplicem visionem triplicem homo accepit oculum sicut dicit Hugo de sancto Victore, scilicet carnis, rationis et contemplationis"; *Breviloquium,* II, c. 12; *Opera Omnia,* t. V. p. 230.

sible to man; it constitutes the object of his search. Because of this we say that the real is rational. It remains true, nevertheless, that everything has its proper value and place in this totality, and it is this fact which makes a partial grasp of reality possible. Many philosophers reach a knowledge of the physical and metaphysical structure of things but fail to discover that profound design which binds all things together: the various kingdoms of the world, the earth and the vast universe of the stars, matter and spirit, creation and its Creator. To fail to discover this is to fail to discover the final cause of things.

This is precisely what happened to Aristotle, who discovered so much about the nature of things and organized all visible reality into an immense system but missed its final purpose because he did not know the relationships which bound creation to God. And because he never arrived at a notion of providence and creation "ex nihilo," he taught the eternity of matter and the world, and the unity of the active intellect. The final result of his research was not truth, as he had proposed, but an ensemble of pernicious errors. His quest began inauspiciously. Aristotle sought the explanation of the world in the world itself. He shattered the totality of the real, and as a result its profound plan escaped him; and with that, its true meaning was also lost.

Plato and Plotinus were wiser. They saw clearly that the explanation of the world must be sought in God. And yet they, too, became entangled in various errors for, deprived of the light of faith, they could not understand how the oneness of God could include multiplicity, that the unity of God does not exclude the Trinity. Further, they taught metempsychosis and hence the self-sufficiency of man in arriving one day at beatitude.

The above line of thought leads unequivocally to the following conclusion: "Philosophical knowledge is the way to the other sciences; but he who wishes to remain in this way falls into darkness."[2] The reason for this failure of philosophy is clearly stated in another passage of St. Bonaventure: "Man before sin had complete knowledge of created things and by this knowledge he was led to God, to praise, adore and love Him: for this was the only purpose of creatures and thus through man they were united to God. But man fell, and having lost this knowledge, there was no one to bring things back to God. Therefore this book, the world, became incomprehensible; the key to its understanding was lost. Hence another book was necessary by which man might be enlightened to grasp the metaphorical meaning of things. This book is Sacred Scripture, which again places before our eyes the analogies and metaphorical properties of the things written in the book of the world. This book of Scripture restores to creatures, so to speak, their voice by which they might make their Lord known, praised and loved. Whence if you ask what value the serpent has for you and how it can serve you, I answer that it has more value for you than the whole world because it teaches you prudence, as the ant teaches you wisdom. Solomon (Prov. 6:6) indeed says: 'Go to the ant, O sluggard . . . and

---

[2] "Philosophica scientia via est ad alias scientias, sed qui ibi vult stare cadit in tenebris."—*De donis Spiritus Sancti,* col. IV, n. 12; *Opera Omnia,* t. V, p. 476.

learn wisdom'; and in Matthew (10:16) it is written: 'Be prudent as serpents.' "[3]

A contemporary reader of the above-cited passage
must find its lines strange and perplexing. It is difficult for him to believe that such statements were
meant to be taken literally. This language goes well
in the field of mysticism but not in philosophy. St.
Bonaventure, nevertheless, was speaking to philosophers and he proposed this manner of thinking as
more true in opposition to that of Aristotle. It is,
therefore, philosophy versus philosophy. In the light
of this, it will be profitable to place in relief the
thoughts which are interwoven in this passage.

The world is a book and things are the words. As
words have value—not inasmuch as they are in themselves beautiful, perfect, solid, of gold or silver, but
inasmuch as they signify concepts—so creatures, although they have consistency and value in themselves, have this only because they bear witness to
man of God and His perfections. As a book is useless
to an illiterate person who sees the letters but does
not comprehend the meaning, so the world loses its
fundamental value when man knows it in itself but
does not perceive its testimony and its significance.
To bear witness and to guide man to God constitutes
not only the value of things but their very truth.
Every science, therefore, even the most profound,
is imperfect and ends in error when it does not grasp
this meaning in the things which it studies.

Man has lost this spiritual vision of reality which
is its most important and authentic aspect. Only
revelation will place him back on the path which

---

[3] *Collationes in Hexaemeron*, XIII, n. 12, p. 390.

will enable him to reacquire it. Philosophy, therefore, must be aided by theology. In this way it will regain the possibility of reaching the end of its journey which is truth. All the human sciences, philosophy included, give us an understanding of things as they are; but only theology tells us why they are such. The former give us *knowledge*, but only the latter leads us to *wisdom*.

The *Reductio artium ad Theologiam* is not merely the devout exercise of a mystic, but the necessary method of every man who sincerely wishes to arrive at truth. It is with good reason that St. Bonaventure, in giving the norms for fruitful study, puts the perfect knowledge of Sacred Scripture in the very first place.

Now, finally, we are in a position to grasp in its full meaning the expression which characterizes the Bonaventurian conception of philosophy, a conception which, as that of St. Anselm, is summed up in the phrase: "Credo ut intelligam"—I believe that I might understand. These thoughts will be clarified in the following chapters.

GOD, THE EXEMPLAR OF CREATURES

The fact that St. Bonaventure refused to recognize the possibility of an autonomous philosophy, which at the same time would be true, must not lead us to believe that his theological works do not contain masterful lines of a rational system of reality. Even within the sphere of theology, when reasoning is introduced it does not cease to be reason, and if philosophy does not comprise the totality of knowledge, it remains nevertheless an important part of human cognition. In the following pages I shall attempt to trace briefly what in my judgment are the essential lines of Bonaventurian philosophy. To say that the thought of Bonaventure is Neo-Platonic is to determine at the same time the logical dynamism which pervades it: a dynamism which goes from God to creatures and, in its second moment, from creatures to God. Our exposition will follow the logical lines of the system.

The Neo-Platonism of St. Bonaventure, as that of St. Augustine, is not so rigorous as to begin immediately from God without prefacing it with a demonstration of His existence. This demonstration is necessary because of the confused state of the human mind which, darkened by the world of the senses, struggles with great difficulty to perceive the very source of its thought.[1]

It is not difficult for man to admit the existence of God. On the contrary, it is impossible for him to deny it. One need only attend to what God is in order to be aware of His existence, which is proclaimed by all that man is and everything that surrounds him. It is God Who renders man and things comprehensible. What indeed is man? He is an intelligence which seeks truth; he is a will which searches for happiness; a being which longs for peace. But man is not satisfied with any particular or partial truth, happiness or peace; he desires the supreme truth, beatitude and peace. Only this can explain his restlessness, his untiring pursuit of one object after another. These are the perfect ideals which attract, set in motion, and drive forward the whole spiritual life of man. Every act of his intellect and will is performed in view of these supreme goals.

To think is to seek the explanation of things, and things are justified not by any cause at all, but

---

[1] "Mira igitur est caecitas intellectus, qui non considerat illud quod prius videt et sine quo nihil potest cognoscere"—*Itinerarium,* c. V, 4; *Opera Omnia,* t. V, p. 309. In every philosophical system the solution of the problem of God is in a strict relationship with its epistemology. The possibility of demonstrating the existence of God depends on His knowability. This is true in a particular way for St. Bonaventure. Hence at this point I should insert at least a short exposition of Bonaventurian epistemology. For the sake of brevity, however, I appeal to the intelligence of the reader which can easily fill in what is lacking here by reading the fifth chapter where the epistemological problem is explicitly treated.

by an absolute cause which is the reason for itself and the source of all explanation. Similarly, to will is merely a surging forward toward the good, a tending to an end. And no good or no end is ever such except in so far as it is absolute and therefore valuable in itself, or in so far as it is a means of attaining the absolute good or end. To deny the existence of the absolute, then, is equivalent to denying the very existence of rational intellection and volition, and hence the very nature of man as such. What is God but the absolute reason and end, the efficient and final cause of all things? Our understanding and willing affirm God's existence, and in the very act of grasping a true understanding of his nature man encounters God's presence. Inversely, our intellect and will exist only inasmuch as there is an absolute God Who attracts and draws it, just as I perform the activity of walking only when there is a goal I wish to reach. As it is impossible not to think and not to will, so it is impossible to deny the exstence of God.

The identical result is obtained if we turn to exterior things and consider them in their metaphysical aspects. Things, for example, are contingent. In themselves they are indifferent to existence or nonexistence; they are in perfect equilibrium between nothingness and being. If they exist it means that someone, who is not contingent and exists necessarily, has caused them to emerge from their indifference and has tipped the balance toward being. All things on reflection reveal complete dependence on some cause; each one of them is an "ens ab alio." Hence their explanation can only be found in a being which is not in its turn "ab alio"; in a being uncreated and eternal. No one, certainly, can give being to himself:

either he has received it from another, or he always had it.

All beings, furthermore, receive perfections and therefore pass from potency to act. This movement would not be possible except for the mediating action of a being already in act. If we can conclude that potency is preceded in the absolute order by act to which potency is subordinated and ordered, then in finding the first act we will discover the explanation for the existence of things. Contingent beings proclaim the existence of necessary being; the "ens ab alio," the existence of the "ens a se." Being in potency points to the existence of pure act. These properties which the world of things demands for their intelligibility, but do not themselves possess, belong exclusively to God. St. Bonaventure treats eight other metaphysical properties of created reality, but it is not necessary to elaborate on them here. The two we have discussed are sufficient to indicate the direction of his thought.

To one familiar with the five ways of St. Thomas, it would seem that in this series of reflections St. Bonaventure is following substantially the same logical procedure as the first three ways of the Angelic Doctor which, taking their point of departure from sensible things, arrive at God by means of the principle of causality. This, however, is only apparently true. All of the Bonaventurian considerations originate, so to speak, from our mind in contact with experience rather than from experience itself.

That knowledge of God, which, as we have seen, stirs up and explains our whole spiritual life and which can be called an innate idea of God,[2] assists us in our intellective acts. When I affirm that the things which have become a part of my experience are contingent, caused, possible, mutable and in potency; when, moreover, I discover their limits, their finiteness and their imperfection I do this because I am looking at them from a superior point of view, and I judge that they lack many possible perfections. "How," observes St. Bonaventure, "could the intellect know that a being is defective and incomplete, if it had no knowledge of a being without any defect?"[3]

The metaphysical aspects of things which we have been considering proclaim the existence of God in the sense that they cause me to perceive that God is present to my mind, and insofar as they determine that confused and indefinite idea which guides every act of my intellect. Rather than demonstrating the existence of God, things bring before my mind the perfections of God and make explicit a certitude which I already find within me. They embellish my initial experience of God. It is precisely here that the Bonaventurian considerations derive their extremely brief structure and their multiplicity in contradistinction to

[2] I shall speak at greater length of this innate idea of God in its proper place and shall attempt to determine its value and character. For the present it is sufficient to observe that for St. Bonaventure an idea is said to be innate, not because we have it in our mind already perfectly formed and detailed, but because it is not derived from experience, although it is developed and determined only when confronted with internal and external experience.

[3] "Quomodo sciret intellectus esse ens defectivum et incompletum, si nullam haberet cognitionem entis absque omni defectu?"—*Itinerarium*, c. III, n. 3; *Opera Omnia*, t. V, p. 304.

the careful dialectical elaborations of St. Thomas' five ways.

These reflections must also be taken into account in order to judge the meaning and the value of the various formulations of St. Anselm's argument with which St. Bonaventure concludes his demonstration of the existence of God. The indubitable truth of the existence of God, observes the Seraphic Doctor, does not result merely from the consideration of the testimony of external existence; it can be discovered in the idea of God itself. God indeed is a being, greater than which cannot be thought. Now a being which cannot be thought of as not existing is in a sense more true than a being which can be thought of as not existing. If, therefore, God is God, i.e., a being than which a more perfect cannot be thought, He cannot be conceived as not existing.

This same line of reasoning is found in St. Augustine's *Soliloquium*: no truth is affirmed except in virtue of the first truth or truth "per essentiam." But the truth through which every other truth is affirmed is undeniable in the highest degree. Therefore, not only is it most certain that God, Supreme Truth, exists, but He is such that nothing can be thought of as more undoubtedly true than He. Hence the existence of God is a truth which cannot be conceived as not true.

The objection commonly advanced against the Anselmian argument is that there is an illegitimate transference from the ideal to the real order. Regardless of what might be said for the argument of St. Anselm, I maintain that this objection does not militate against the reasoning of St. Bonaventure. The idea of God, from which he takes his point of departure, is not an idea formed by my mind nor by the mind of any man. It is an idea which is imposed on the mind and grasped in the vital activity of human thought. It bears witness to a real presence which is the source of my power to think. In this sense it does not depend on my mind; rather it is superior to it. In Bonaventurian thought, therefore, a reality is not inferred from an idea. On the contrary, a reality is discovered which underlies and is manifested through an idea, in which, so to speak, this reality acts.

No man can seriously deny the existence of God since he thinks and judges in virtue of God's presence, and in this sense experiences Him. The denials of atheists and the errors of idolators can only be explained by the false concept which they have of God and which they apply to things that cannot at all be God. These things they would have take the place of God in their system of reality.

What we usually call demonstrations of the existence of God are simply reflections, the purpose of which is to form a correct concept of God within us, to determine more exactly the confused idea we have of Him. "Arguments of this kind are exercises of the intellect rather than proofs giving evidence and manifesting the truth as proven."[4]

All of the preceding considerations tell us that God is the Supreme Being, being *par excellence,* the sum of being; thus confirming perfectly the name which God gives to Himself in Sacred Scripture: "I am who

---

[4] Unde huiusmodi ratiocinationes potius sunt quaedam exercitationes intellectus, quam rationes dantes evidentiam et manifestantes ipsum verum probatum."—*De Mysterio Trinitatis,* q. I, a. I, ad 12; *Opera Omnia,* t. V, p. 51.

am"—I am being *(esse)*. For St. Bonaventure also, this is the radical attribute of God from which the mind of man can deduce His other attributes with facility; the vantage point from which man can more easily penetrate to some degree the abyss of the divine essence.

The finest example of this deductive process, outstanding for its simplicity and dialectical power, is the fifth chapter of the *Itinerarium* which synthesizes in a few pages the most sublime human speculations with regard to the divine attributes. The being which is such in the purest, simplest and most absolute sense of the term, is also first, eternal, most simple, most actual, most perfect and supremely one. These attributes flow one from another with rigorous logical necessity.

Clearly there can be nothing anterior to being, for nothing can exist except being: therefore being is absolutely *first*. But if it is absolutely first it is necessarily *eternal* for it is contradictory that it begin to be, since there is nothing anterior to it to bring it into existence nor can it bring itself into existence since it would thus be before it existed. It is therefore without a beginning and, as a consequence, *most simple*. Everything which is in any manner composite depends on the principles or elements which compose it. But God, first and eternal, excludes all dependence and hence any sort of composition, as also any shadow of potentiality. His absolute independence as regards His operations flows from the fact that beings in potency depend on a being in act. God, then, is *most actual* or pure act and at the same time *most perfect* since He lacks nothing. This latter flows from the former—His perfection from His actuality—for nothing can be added to Him, since as we have said above, He excludes every shadow of potentiality.

From these perfections another derives: the supreme unity, or the necessary uniqueness of God. God is absolutely first, eternal, most simple, most actual, most perfect, and this with regard to all other beings. Another being equal to God is unthinkable because its existence would completely destroy all these perfections.

The deduction of the divine perfections continues. Each one of the perfections calls forth another corresponding to it and at first sight apparently contradictory to it. By the very fact that God is absolutely first, He is also absolutely *last*. Since He is the first of all beings He does all things for Himself; what did not exist could not be the object of His operations. He is, then, necessarily the ultimate end of all things as well as their beginning; He is the alpha and omega of reality. Further, because He is eternal He is also most present. Eternity excludes any temporal development. God has no beginning nor does He progress from one state to another. All of these things are contradictory to eternity. God, therefore, excluding all beginning has neither past nor future; He is always present. Absolute simplicity in its turn has another facet: supreme greatness. Since God is perfectly simple in essence, He is everything that He has, i.e., He possesses them essentially. Now everything which one possesses essentially is possessed without limits. Thus we conclude that the perfections of God are infinite.

Activity and immutability also appear contradictory, for it would seem that he who acts at the same time moves. Nevertheless in God supreme activity and supreme immutability coincide. Since God is most actual, He is pure act and hence excludes all potency and as a consequence all change, for in acting He neither acquires nor loses anything. The operation of God is so perfect that in one single act He brings about all that He would, and hence His act is always identical. Furthermore, God is most perfect—without limitation—and therefore He is *immense*. Nothing can be thought of more excellent and greater than God.

Because God is the One *par excellence,* He is omnifarious or "ens omnimodum." All multiplicity derives from unity, and because God is pure unity He is the principle of all multiplicity. Certainly He is not the essence of all things, but He is the most perfect, most universal and most sufficient cause of all essences. He is, in other words, the efficient, exemplary and final cause of all things. He is omnipotent, omniscient and good in all modes and under all aspects.

This page of Bonaventurian thought which I have attempted to interpret here must not be forgotten, both because of its theoretical value as a most sublime metaphysical meditation and because of its historical value. It will be most useful to have at hand when beginning to read, the profound pages written by the Neo-Platonists of the Renaissance, starting with the first book of the *De docta ignorantia* of Cardinal Nicholas of Cusa.

It still remains for us to develop the last remarks and to study the relative attributes of God—those attributes which will explain how imperfect and limited beings can have their origin in God, the Supreme and Infinite Being, and how multiplicity can proceed from unity. For St. Bonaventure this is the metaphysical problem *par excellence:* "Our whole metaphysics is concerned with emanation, exemplarism and the final end of things, namely, to be enlightened by spiritual rays and to return on high. Thus you will be a true metaphysician."[5]

We can consider the problem in four moments or aspects as formulated in the following questions: 1. How is it possible for multiplicity to proceed from unity? 2. Does it proceed directly or indirectly? necessarily or freely? 3. What value do these manifold things have with regard to unity? Or in less technical words, what is the fundamental significance of created things? 4. How does multiplicity return to unity? It is evident that the answers to these questions flow logically one from another: the second from the first; the third from the first and second; and the fourth from the other three. The study of the relative attributes of God which constitutes the last part of this chapter will enable us to answer the first question. We shall be concerned with three divine attributes which for St. Bonaventure are the key to understanding how God could create: omnipotence, wisdom, and goodness.

The first step from unity to multiplicity, the first explanation of creation, consists in the word. Scripture and patristic tradition permit St. Bonaventure to follow the Neo-Platonic scheme according to which the first degree of emanation is the intellect, or the *logos*. God, the most perfect being, must know Himself adequately before all else. All knowledge comes about through assimilation, that is, by means of a

---

[5] "Haec est tota nostra metaphysica: de emanatione, de exemplaritate, de consummatione, scilicet illuminari per radios spirituales et reduci ad summum. Et sic eris verus metaphisicus." *Collationes in Hexaemeron*, III, n. 2; *Opera Omnia*, t. V, p. 343.

"similitudo" which is formed in the one knowing.
Through this "similitudo" he who knows seeks to re-
produce, to generate in himself the object known.
Let us raise this to the infinite and we shall succeed
in catching a glimpse of how the idea of "similitudo,"
which God, with His infinitely perfect cognitive act,
generates of Himself, must be another Self: the Word
consubstantial with the Father. Nothing is more like
a thing than the thing itself. It is evident that at this
point St. Bonaventure has already gone beyond Neo-
Platonism which held that the intellect was inferior
to God.

God would not know His divine essence adequately, however, if He did not know everything that He
could do. Hence it is necessary to affirm that the
word, the "similitudo expressiva" of God, is at the
same time the "similitudo expressiva" of all real and
possible things which have in the word or the divine
idea their eternal likeness, their eternal "similitudo"
or "ratio," their idea or exemplar.

This doctrine which is common to all Christian
thought, at least from Augustine on, assumes an
original characteristic in St. Bonaventure, and it is
worthwhile noting, since it constitutes the interior
dynamism of his thought. Certainly God did not
bring into being all the possible ways in which His
essence could be imitated. But with the word and in
the word and through the word He produces the
"rationes" of all things. Expressing Himself in the
word, God also expresses all real and possible things.
This point must be kept in mind because it will help
us to understand many statements of St. Bonaventure,
especially the one which proclaims the necessary
mediation of the word in explaining and compre-

hending creation.[6] Here we have the key which will resolve the difficulties which prevented Aristotle from attributing to God the knowledge of things of this world and impeded Plotinus from grasping the complete equality of the intellect with God. To Aristotle it seemed that the knowledge of diverse and mutable things would be contradictory to God's immutability; Plotinus thought that the knowledge of multiple things would itself involve a certain multiplicity.

St. Bonaventure, in answer to Aristotle, observes it is true that all knowledge is impossible if the knower cannot acquire the "similitudo" of the thing known; it is necessary to understand in the "similitudo." When I affirm that one thing is like another, I can mean either that both have a common quality or that one is an imitation of the other, or that the first is the pattern of the second. Clearly it cannot be said that God possesses the "similitudines" of things in the first two meanings. For the first would destroy the absolute transcendence of God, which excludes any metaphysical univocity with the being of creatures. The second possibility argues against God's immutability as Aristotle had observed. The third meaning, however, offers no repugnance, nor does it even involve an imperfection (divine knowledge does not depend on things, but things depend on God's knowledge); it is entirely proper to the divine perfection. Indeed, He would be a poor kind of God Who could not know anything except Himself.

The reasoning of Plotinus is no less unfortunate.

---

[6] "Horum ostium est intellectus Verbi incarnati, qui est radix intelligentiae omnium; unde qui non habet hoc ostium, intrare non potest." *Collationes in Hexaemeron,* III, n. 4; *Opera Omnia,* t. V. p. 343.

The multiplicity of things is not reflected in the Word: it does not enter, so to speak, into Him. The ideas in the mind of God appear as a multiplicity only to him who looks at the problem externally, not to him who views it from within. As we saw in our earlier discussion of the divine perfections, simplicity includes the greatest actuality and perfection. Now the greater the number of things an idea makes known, the more perfect it is; and the greater the number of things a word expresses, the more perfect the word is. Hence the supreme perfection of the divine knowledge requires that God know all things in one most perfect idea; that He express the infinity of possible things in one most perfect word.

From this point of view it is not difficult to understand how God knows the mutable immutably, how He knows infallibly what is free, "incausabiliter" what is caused, eternally what is in time. In short, how He knows the multiple in one most simple act. In the divine wisdom the multiple finds its primary foundation: it is thought in the mind of God. It is the first step toward reality, although its reality is not yet accomplished.

In order to explain the passage from possibility to being, from conception to realization, it is necessary both that God be able to bring it about and that He will to bring it about. But does God have this power? Is not such a voluntary act contradictory to His nature? There seem to be various reasons which indicate that God cannot act on anything other than Himself. He cannot act on another thing without transferring His own power to it. If God were to act outside of Himself, His power would no longer coincide with His essence and hence He could no longer be said to be simple. Furthermore, the agent depends in some manner on the term of his action, inasmuch as he is limited by it. The presence of the term is the necessary condition for a power to act. All of these things seem repugnant to divine power.

St. Bonaventure begins by observing that if God did not have the power to create, to act outside of Himself or "ad extra," namely, if He did not have some things other than Himself as the term of His action, He would be less perfect than creatures: than man, for example, who produces innumerable things by his skill. It is not true, furthermore, that to have something other than oneself as the term of one's action always involves that dependence and indigence which we spoke of above. When God acts He is totally wherever He acts since He is immense and, as a result, most intimate to the thing which is the term of His action. Because He is the most perfect efficient cause, His very action and presence constitute the thing itself. He does not have to overcome any distance between Himself and the object of His activity. He acts only to give and not to receive. He acts without dependence; He needs the help of nothing.

The power to create, then, is demanded by the perfection of God, nor does it contain any imperfection. It is clearly most possible for God to manifest Himself in all His magnificence and to fill the metaphysical void of nothingness with the variety of beings. Only one thing escapes the divine power: the irrational and all else which in some way involves a contradiction or is repugnant to God's perfection. The irrational and evil can be reduced to *nothing,* which, as such, cannot be the term of any power.

The intrinsic possibility of things finds its basis in

the divine wisdom. Their extrinsic possibility has its foundation in God's supreme power. But only the most holy will of God gives us the reason for their actual existence and, therefore, it is to His will that we attribute causality with regard to creatures. Certainly the cause of things, observes the Seraphic Doctor at this point, is the divine essence which in its most simple unity blends together an infinite sea of perfections. Nevertheless, our imperfect manner of expressing ourselves—because of which we distinguish wisdom, power, goodness, in God—is not in error, since it is true that God is wise, powerful, good, and the like. It must not be forgotten, however, that the divine perfections are one with His essence. And when it is said that the cause of things is the divine will, it is to be understood as referring to God insofar as He wills. But why should God have willed to create the world? Was He not most perfect and happy without creation? The explanation is found in the nature of the will which is nothing else but the manifestation of goodness.[7]

The good tends by its nature to diffuse itself, and at the same time it is the end of all things. Thus the good is the center and source of both a centrifugal and centripetal dynamism. If the good were only "diffusivum sui," its diffusion would be natural, necessary and blind. But on the other hand, because it is the end of all things, this diffusion finds its explanation and hence its rationality in the good itself. The will is precisely that act by which the good reflects

---

[7] "Ratio autem, quare voluntati attribuitur causalitas haec est, quia ratio causando est bonitas et in ratione effective." *In I. Sent.*, d. XLV, a. II, q. I; ed. minor., t. I, p. 639.

upon itself and recognizes itself as the end of its own diffusion. The will, then, unites the efficient and final cause in itself and from this union every rational action arises. Why did God create? Why did He give other beings a share in existence? Because He, essential Goodness, tends to diffuse Himself, to communicate to other beings all the goodness of which they are capable.

But what is the end of creation? The end of creation is the glory of God. The gift which God has given to creatures is not a capricious gift, a pure manifestation of an infinite superabundance of good. Creatures find the reason for their existence in the fact that they are called to tend to the Supreme Good — the "Summun Bonum" — as the object of their knowledge, their admiration and their love. For St. Bonaventure the divine will has within itself the impulse and the pattern of its action, and is a necessary synthesis of both. This must be kept in mind when speaking of Bonaventurian voluntarism. The being which at the beginning of our study appeared as necessarily existing now reveals itself to us in the nature of the good, and therefore "diffusivum sui."

As the concept of necessary being or "ens a se" helped us to understand that the perfection of the divine essence is possible, so the concept of the Supreme Good helps us to understand the divine action, from those necessary and ineffable actions "ad intra" —in which the Supreme Good is communicated perfectly and eternally from the Father to the Son and from both to the Holy Spirit—to His actions "ad extra." Creation indeed appears to us as a further diffusion of goodness, the possibility and the measure of which God sees eternally in the Word.

EXEMPLARISM IN CREATION

The examination of the solution which St. Bonaventure gives to the second and third moment of the complex problem of the relationship between unity and multiplicity, between God and creation—the fundamental problem of metaphysics—will form the object of this chapter. It will naturally be divided into two parts.

How do things proceed from God? Necessarily or freely? Directly or indirectly? Totally or only in part? It is easily seen that all Greek philosophy from Thales to Plotinus was concerned with this problem. The solutions were many but none of them completely fulfilled the requirements of consistency and philosophical truth. The solution to which accurate and careful philosophical reflection must lead is what the simple faithful learn in their catechism: the world comes forth from God Who has created it *freely* and *from nothing*.

This answer is a logical consequence of what was said in the last part of the preceding chapter. The principal difficulties which prevented the pagan philosophers from perceiving the complete truth when confronted with this problem are evident; in fact, we have already noted some of them. Plato, Aristotle and Plotinus never succeeded in overcoming Greek dualism. They were convinced that an agent could act only on some pre-existing matter; that at least prime matter, together with God, must be eternal. Another error common to all the Greek philosophers with regard to creation was that they could not conceive multiplicity as a free emanation from unity. If God has produced things, He could only have produced them by a natural—and hence necessary—act of the divine essence, as it is natural for man to generate another man. The Greeks arrived at a conception of God as the Supreme Good, Pure Act and most Simple Unity, but they did not succed in understanding Him as Sovereign Love. From this twofold source derive the uncertainty of the nature of the Platonic *Demiurge* placed between the world of ideas and the chaos of matter, the inaccessibility and solitude of Aristotle's *Unmoved Mover,* and the necessity of the hierarchical emanation of Plotinus.

If the world proceeds naturally from God, one can understand Plato's position that in order to explain the existence of things it is necessary to admit a world of perfect forms as the source of sensible reality. Everything which is produced by natural generation comes from something like itself—a man from a man, a horse from a horse. Hence to explain the origin of each series of things generated, it is necessary to posit an ungenerated form.

Aristotle did well when he pointed out the groundlessness of the Platonic world of ideas. But he, in his turn, was unable to attain the complete comprehension of God's manner of acting, which, precisely because it is most perfect, is absolutely other than that which we observe in created beings. When he denies knowledge of the world to God and upholds the impossibility of God having made things in order to safeguard His immutability, Aristotle reduces the action of God to the level of acting we see in nature. He did not understand that the knowledge of God does not depend on things, but rather things depend on the divine ideas. He did not perceive that God, in knowing all the possibles "ab aeterno," also willed "ab aeterno" to call into existence those which He had chosen by an inscrutable decree of His free and most holy will. Creation does not imply any change in God. God has created things in the manner of a most perfect and prolific artist, who has always willed to realize some of His ideal conceptions. It is clear that for such an artist, the external existence of his works of art modifies neither his knowledge nor his creative will. The change is entirely external; it takes place only in the work of art and not in the mind of the artist.

The second difficulty which beset Aristotle can also be shown to lack consistency if we place the action of God on its proper level, which is that of supreme perfection. The Stagirite cannot be shaken from his position based on the philosophical adage, "ex nihilo nihil fit." According to this conception, an action cannot be placed without a pre-existing term to which the action extends. What Aristotle did not grasp is that a most perfect agent is not subject to this law. In what would God's infinite perfection consist if not in acting without encumbrance, without dependence of any sort, and hence without a pre-existing term. God does not perceive an already existing term; He places it and creates it in the act itself. This thought must be insisted upon and is well worth clarifying.

Let us consider these two statements: first, he who produces a thing is the more perfect inasmuch as the influence which he exercises on it and the imprint

which he leaves there is greater. Second, he who acts
is the more perfect the more he can act by himself
and the less he depends on other things. Paganini
never showed the greatness of his prodigious genius
more than when he continued a concert with only
one string remaining on his violin. If the perfection
of someone's work is greater, the fewer the things are
that he needs for it, then God is the infinitely perfect
agent because He needs nothing. He is a Paganini
who goes to the concert without a violin and at the
opportune moment He causes it to leap out of nothingness. Creation "ex nihilo" is, then, demanded by
the infinite perfection of the divine operation. When
God acts "ad extra," He creates. He needs absolutely
nothing; not even prime matter. He creates not only
the things themselves, but even their principles.

Having arrived at this point, we have also uncov-
ered the other error of Greek philosophy and of Aristotle in particular: the eternity of the world. St.
Bonaventure was always a bitter adversary of this
opinion. While for St. Thomas the possibility of a
world created "ab aeterno" could not be excluded by
force of logic alone, the Seraphic Doctor judged it
to be contradictory;[1] and this principally because of
two considerations.

Once it has been established that the world was
created by God "ex nihilo," creation "ab aeterno"
becomes inconceivable. The word "ex" has only two

---

[1] ". . . Ponere mundum aeternum esse ponendo res
omnes ex nihilo productas . . . omnino est contra
veritatem et rationem . . . ut nullum philosophorum
quantumcumque parvi intellectus crediderim hoc
posuisse." *In II Sent.*, d. I, pars. I, a. I, q. 2; *Opera
Omnia*, t. II, p. 22.

possible significations: either it indicates the matter of which a thing is made, or its origin—the point from which it comes into existence. The first meaning is excluded by the preceding discussion. Only the second signification remains. If the nothingness of things has preceded the being of things, one can say that the being of things has had an absolute beginning. Every beginning, however, is irreconcilable with eternity.

The eternity of the world, furthermore, brings with it inadmissible consequences. The world without man has no meaning, for all things are ordered immediately to man, and only through man to God. Thus, if the world is eternal, it is necessary to admit that an infinite number of men have existed and, therefore, an infinite number of souls presently exist since souls are incorruptible forms. But the simultaneous existence of an infinite number of things is generally agreed to be inconceivable since an infinite number is a contradiction in terms. In order to escape this contradiction, either one must admit, as Plato did, the transmigration of souls, or affirm, as Aristotle did, that there is only one immortal soul for all men. These are inadmissible solutions, especially for Christians, inasmuch as one could no longer speak of eternal reward or punishment, thus destroying the notion of morality itself.

The eternity of the world becomes comprehensible only if one admits the eternity of matter. Let us take an illustration. If there existed an eternal foot which pressed down on a layer of eternal dust, the imprint of the foot, although produced, would be coeternal with the foot. Things are imprints of God—"vestigia Dei." They would be as eternal as God only if an eternal matter existed which receives them. Since, however, matter is created, it has also had a beginning, and every presupposition which would render things in any way eternal vanishes.

The same observation applies also to Plotinus' doctrine of emanation which was taken up again by the Arabians. Once the eternity of matter is admitted, one can no longer speak of a true *creation* but only of a formation of the world. A formation which God could well entrust to created intelligences since only the creative act belongs exclusively to God. It must be added, however, that if Neo-Platonism becomes comprehensible when the eternity of matter is admitted, it is still based on an erroneous principle: that because God is perfectly simple He can produce only a unique effect. But as we saw in the preceding chapter, His simplicity involves a most perfect actuality and infinite richness.

Philosophy, then, obliges us to subscribe to the Christian teaching that God has created the world from nothing, freely and directly, after having conceived it eternally in the Word and willed it as a manifestation of His divine liberality.

What value and meaning does creation have in relation to God? This question can be understood in two senses. We understand it in the first and more obvious sense when we ask the further question: What is the end of creation? In this case the answer has already been given at the end of the last chapter where it was shown that, if the goodness of God is the center of diffusion for created things, it is also the necessary center of attraction. God could create only to manifest His goodness: hence creatures are ordered by their very nature to proclaim the glory of God—

the immensity of His perfections. He is their supreme Good.

It is the question taken in its second sense, however, which shall be treated in the last part of this chapter. In order to understand this second meaning with suitable clarity, certain considerations must be called to mind. God is the infinitely perfect being—total being. Creatures also are beings. These two statements seem to contradict each other. Either it is true that God is being in all its fullness, and then creatures must be reduced to mere appearances which cannot possess anything of being in themselves, or the second alternative is true that creatures possess being and in this case God is not total being for its totality would be the sum of the being of both God and creatures.

The dilemma is not as cogent as it seems, however. There is a way out and it is the way of analogy. The being of God and the being of creatures are on two different planes: the first is original being in all its fullness and truth; the being of creatures is being only by participation, by imitation, by a likeness to that of the divine. With this, not only is the second meaning of the question with which we started clarified, but we already have the answer: creatures participate in being; they are constituted in reality as imitations and images of God. Indeed, God is not only the efficient and final cause of creation; He is also its exemplary cause.

Up to this point, St. Bonaventure has been merely repeating the unanimous teaching of all Christian thinkers. From here on he follows his own path, although a large part of it has already been traced by St. Augustine and his greatest mediaeval disciples. The personal development which St. Bonaventure gives to Christian metaphysics consists in emphasizing the role of exemplarism in the network of relations which exist between God and creation.

We have seen previously that for the Seraphic Doctor the primary foundation of creation is found precisely in the fact that God in knowing Himself expresses in His most perfect idea the "rationes," the eternal patterns of all possible things. For this reason He is necessarily the exemplary cause of all things created and creatable. In a corresponding fashion things are neither possible nor realizable except as copies and imitations of God. As a consequence the value and fundamental significance of things will consist precisely in being images of God.[2] To discover the modes, the measure, and the laws of exemplarism is the principal task of the metaphysician who searches for the profound structure of reality.

The first question which arises is: what is the essence of the image? The similarity between two things does not suffice to constitute one thing the image of the other. Two eggs, for example, of the same size and color are very similar to each other, but it cannot properly be said that one is the image of the other. In order for one thing to be called an image of the other it is necessary that the former be produced in imitation of the latter. This is the case with created beings which are produced and, in a wide sense, generated by God in imitation of Himself. Both the mystic, who transfigures things in his loving impetuosity, and the metaphysician must assert that crea-

---

[2] ". . . omnis enim creatura ex natura est illius aeternae sapientiae quaedam effigies et similitudo." *Itinerarium,* c. II, n. 12; *Opera Omnia,* t. V, p. 303.

tion is essentially a book which tells us of God.

These statements can be given an incorrect meaning. They can be understood in the sense that the whole consistency of creatures is found precisely in their manifesting God. In this case they are nothing but signs or symbols of God and this relation of manifesting has no other foundation than God Himself. Thus we would become entangled in the pantheistic idealism of Berkeley. It must not be forgotten that God, in manifesting Himself in creation, creates, meaning that He communicates or gives being to things through which they first of all exist and then are images of God. Although being images is essential to them, nevertheless their essence does not completely consist in being images. Their relationship of similarity to God is certainly an essential relation, but it is always a relation inconceivable without an absolute "quid" as a foundation. Their own being is so concrete that they can be known—and therefore have their truth—even without adverting to their relation of manifesting God. It always remains true, however, that the complete intelligibility and rationality of creatures are attained only when this relation is discovered and becomes clear to the mind of the investigator.

In knowing things, it is possible to stop at the things themselves, satisfied with the wonders which the study of their structure reveals. But it is possible, on the other hand, to go beyond them and arrive at God, following the invitation which things themselves give to us. Clearly, whoever stops at things condemns himself to giving them a definitive value which they do not have and hence ends up by becoming ensnared in innumerable errors. "Either one stops amid the beauty of creatures or through it he passes beyond. The first is the way of error."[3] It is precisely the mistake of the natural philosophers—"naturalium philosophorum"—to use the expression of St. Bonaventure.

All things bear in themselves and disclose to him who can see it a certain resemblance to God. The universe, however, is most varied and ordered in an almost infinite hierarchy from the lowest to the most perfect. And each order in its own way imitates the divine perfections. It is impossible to even consider determining the manner and degree of similarity which each expresses. It is possible, however, to distinguish things according to the perfection and the efficacy with which they express this resemblance to God.

St. Bonaventure distinguishes three different degrees of resemblance: the "umbra," the "vestigium," and the "imago," arranged in the progressive order of their efficacy. The "umbra" is a very remote and confused resemblance to God; in the "vestigium" the resemblance is still remote but it is distinct; the "imago" is a close and distinct resemblance. Things are a shadow or "umbra" of God insofar as they are referred back to God as their general cause and manifest the attributes of God common to the three persons of the Most Holy Trinity. They are a trace or "vestigium" of God inasmuch as they are referred back to God as their efficient, exemplary and final cause, and hence they manifest the attributes appro-

[3] "Aut sistitur in pulchritudine creaturae, aut per illam tenditur in aliud. Si primo modo tunc est via deviationis." *In I Sent.*, d. 3, pars I, a. unicus, q. 2, ad 1; *Opera Omnia,* t. I, p. 72.

priated to each of the three persons: omnipotence to the Father, wisdom to the Son, and goodness to the Holy Spirit. Those creatures are images of God which have God as their object and lead to a knowledge of the attributes proper to each of the three persons. All things are an "umbra" and "vestigium" of God, but only spiritual beings are in addition an "imago." It remains for us to point out the philosophical richness of this doctrine, which at first sight appears to be merely the loving reflections of a mystic.

To know how things have been made and to understand the laws governing their activity is certainly to have a solid and precious knowledge of them. But to succeed in comprehending why they have been made thus and why they act according to given laws is to have a much more perfect knowledge of them. It is precisely to this more perfect knowledge that the doctrine of universal analogy carries us. The application of this method which helps us to uncover the truth by the logic of analogy is met with at every step in the works of St. Bonaventure. He develops this logic with a sureness and richness which cannot but appear strange and marvelous to us moderns.

All bodies, notwithstanding their infinite variety, agree in this that all have a certain dimension which places them and limits them in space; a disposition of parts regulated according to a certain order, and an intrinsic tendency which determines their actions and constitutes their weight. All bodies are composed according to this threefold law of measure, order and weight. There is a reason for this, but how can we discover it? It is sufficient to call to mind that creation is, as it were, the fruit of the power, wisdom and goodness of God, in order to perceive that weight, order and measure are the necessary imprints of God inasmuch as He is their efficient cause through His power, their exemplary cause through His wisdom, and their final cause through His goodness. Measure is, at it were, the power of the body; the internal order of its parts is its truth or intelligibility; and the weight is its goodness or value.

If we attempt to search more intimately into the nature of bodies, we shall be forced to recognize that their essence is constituted by the substantial union of two principles: matter and form. Matter is the essential foundation, the form is the expression, and the substantial union is the rich bond of their being. Whoever has discovered this structure in corporeal beings is led to wonder why the constitutive laws of bodies are based on these three principles. It is impossible to find the answer without taking into account the creative Trinity Whose traces are found in every being. The matter insofar as it is the essential foundation of corporeal being foreshadows the Father; the form inasmuch as it is the expression of the reality of corporeal being foreshadows the Son; the substantial bond which binds matter and form together foreshadows the Holy Spirit.

Another incontrovertible testimony is the existence of corporeal and spiritual beings. We wish not only to state but to understand why rational beings exist together with irrational beings. It is not difficult. God indeed has created in order to diffuse and to manifest His goodness. To accomplish this end it is not sufficient that some beings exist which bear in themselves a trace and imprint of the divine perfections. It is also necessary that there exist other beings who, besides bearing this resemblance, can recognize and appreciate in themselves and in other things this constitutional analogy with the supreme Being, and who desire that this analogy become always clearer and more expressive—some beings, in short, which recognize God as their proper model and strive to become even more faithful copies. Only in this way is the exigency of the infinite goodness of God satisfied. In desiring to communicate His goodness in creation He must also will that creatures be ordered to Himself, recognizing Him and loving Him as the Supreme Good. It is clear that if irrational creatures are capable of receiving the communications of God, only rational creatures, through understanding and love, can lead themselves and other things back to God. It is in this that rationality properly consists.

It is evident, furthermore, that the resemblance which rational creatures have to God is much more perfect than that of other things. It reproduces in itself not only the analogy with a perfection of God, but analogy of the very life of God insofar as it is destined to know and to desire, according to its capacity, what God Himself knows and loves. For what is creation if it is not the fruit of the knowledge and love which God has for Himself. The likeness to God, which the rational creature has, can—precisely because it is vital—be lived with greater or lesser intensity and can even, in a certain sense, die. This happens when man, taken up with the beauty of creatures, forgets the Creator, arrests within himself that spontaneous movement of the mind and heart which leads him back to God, the Supreme Truth, Beauty and Goodness, and refuses to develop his native capacity of conforming himself more and more to God until he becomes His expressed image.

That the life of the soul is analogous to the life of God is seen more clearly in the intrinsic structure of the soul than in the relationships which bind it to all creation. The soul is composed of memory, intellect and will. The memory insofar as it contains within itself the ideas and offers them to the contemplation of the intelligence reduces the intellect to act; the latter expresses these ideas in a word. From knowledge, the product of the memory and intellect, proceeds desire and love. Analogously the Father generates the Son, Who is His expressed eternal knowledge, and from both proceeds the Holy Spirit. In God there is unity of essence and distinction of Persons; in the soul there is unity of essence and distinction of acts.

Is it possible for the creature to be likened even more expressly to God? Yes, given the case that God is pleased to communicate to the creature not merely analogous being and perfection, but His very life. Something of the divine then enters the creature, which becomes capable not only of conforming itself to God but of entering into friendship with Him. That divine gift raises the creature, so to speak, to the level of the divine without, of course, causing him to become God—a thing absurd and impossible. This miracle of condescension on the part of God, and of grandeur on the part of the creature, is accomplished by grace, which makes the human soul not only an image but a "similitudo" of God. The similitude is distinguished from the image in this that the similitude demands something common to the two things. Grace is properly a participation by man in the divine nature. It is a participation which renders us capable and worthy of entering into society with God;

it renders us deiform—as like God as possible for him who is not and cannot be God. With grace, which is a seed which shall flower fully in glory, man attains the supreme goal of his capacity for God, his restlessness and inclination toward Him.

We can conclude from our brief study that while the other mediaeval masters preferred to study the rapport between things and God considered as the efficient and final cause of creation, St. Bonaventure made God the object of his philosophical meditation, especially in so far as He is the exemplary cause of creation. Thus the Seraphic Doctor has given us a metaphysics of exemplarism in perfect harmony with the Platonic-Augustinian tendency of his thought. This doctrine has permitted St. Bonaventure to become the "philosophical consciousness" of St. Francis, to use the expression of Father Gemelli.[4] It translates into philosophical language the poetry of the "Canticle of Creatures."

[4] Agostino Gemelli, *Il Francescanesimo*, ediz. 1, Milano, Vita e Pensiero, 1932, p. 57.

THE STRUCTURE OF THE CREATURE

In order to understand how the reversion of multiplicity to unity, namely, the return of the creature to God, is accomplished, it is necessary to know the structure of reality—the structure which will reveal to us the metaphysical rhythm with which things return to God as their complement and final cause. In this chapter we shall treat of the essential lines of Bonaventurian cosmology, and in the following chapter those of his psychology.

The Seraphic Doctor explains his cosmological ideas in several questions of the *Commentary on the Sentences:* questions which are meant to be a theologico-philosophical explanation of the biblical account of creation. Naturally his cosmology moves in the atmosphere of the astronomical and physical knowledge of his time with the necessary adaptation to his metaphysics. It is not our purpose to attempt the complete reconstruction of the system of the world according to Bonaventurian thought. I shall deal instead only with those themes which, being especially metaphysical, have theoretical as well as historical value.

The universe, at the summons of the divine word, did not spring into being from nothing, in as perfect and ordered a state as it appeared to the sight of the first man. For although the divine power was certainly capable of accomplishing this, nevertheless the creation and ordering of the world was effected according to a progressive plan explicitly sketched in the six days of the biblical account. At the first moment God created the angels, the empyrean, matter and time: the first spiritual nature, the first principles of corporeal nature and the first measure of all things.[1] The Bonaventurian conception of the empyrean is far removed from our modern notion of the heavens. It is a most luminous body which is above the crystalline heavens and the firmanent or sidereal heavens. It was destined to be the place of the angels and beatified men. It is a body, however, in which matter is reduced to the minimum possible in such manner that it can scarcely be called a body. It is almost all form and, as a consequence, most active and luminous. The empyrean is the perfect opposite of the matter created at the first moment of creation which was united to a most imperfect form hardly sufficient to make it exist in its obscure and inert uniformity.

In this first step of Bonaventurian cosmology it can already be seen that he substantially accepts the Aristotelian thesis which points to matter and form as the ultimate principles of corporeal reality. This agreement between St. Bonaventure and Aristotle, however, must not deceive us or make us less intent on

---

[1] "Quatuor fuerint primo creata, scilicet caelum empyreum, natura angelica, materia et tempus: . . . prima inter substantias spirituales est angelus, prima inter substantias corporales activas est empyreum et prima inter passivas est materia elementorum, et prima inter mensuras est tempus." *In II Sent.*, d. 2, pars 1, a. 2, q. 3; *Opera Omnia*, t. II, p. 68.

gathering the original development of his thought. It would not be wise for us to pass over the most notable differences which exist between the two cosmologies.

To begin with, while Aristotle admits the composition of matter and form in material things only, St. Bonaventure attributes it to spiritual substances also—the angels and the human soul. Evidently the two thinkers have different concepts of matter. Matter, the Seraphic Doctor teaches, can be considered with two mentalities: either with the mentality of the physicist or that of the metaphysician. The physicist considers matter as the subject of all the substantial and accidental changes which come about in bodies; as the invariable "quid" which makes all the variations possible by receiving them. The metaphysician pushes his consideration further. He insists on the concept of matter as lacking all form; pure potency without a shadow of act except, of course, that act which makes it to be matter. The metaphysician considers the *essence* of matter, which is absolute indifference to every form, spiritual and corporeal, while the physicist's consideration stops at the concrete being of matter with which it presents itself. He sees, therefore, a matter already actuated and bound to a corporeal form.

It is no wonder, then, that the physicist refuses to admit matter in spirits: his matter cannot be found in spiritual substances precisely because it is corporeal. The metaphysician, on the other hand, must always affirm that where there is potency, there is matter, and that every being which in some manner can be thought of as deprived of a due perfection partakes of the essence of matter. No creature can completely escape this law. Pure actuality without a mixture of potency is the privilege of the necessary and immutable being. Metaphysical matter cannot exist by itself because it is only a principle of being, while physical matter can exist by itself since it is already actuated by a corporeal form. At this point we can see that the matter created by God as one of the principles of the world is properly physical matter; it corresponds to the earth "inanis and vacua" of Sacred Scripture. St. Bonaventure calls it "materia informis," not because it was completely lacking in form, but because this first form was incomplete. It left matter undetermined with regard to all the forms of bodies, although conferring on it an act of existence already determined in contradistinction to metaphysical matter but undetermined with regard to every act of existence, spiritual and corporeal.

Once again we must state that St. Bonaventure is far removed from the Aristotelian line of thought. For Aristotle and his school the form gives complete actuation to the matter which it informs. As a consequence every body owes its perfection to one unique form. St. Thomas, for example, is in accord with St. Bonaventure in admitting that creation was accomplished according to a progressive plan. But the chaos or earth "inanis et vacua" was not, for St. Thomas, the "materia informis" of the Seraphic Doctor but, rather, a combination of the four simple elements which were already well determined, elements to which—according to the physical opinions of that time—all the variety of bodies could be reduced: earth, water, air and fire. A matter which would be corporeal without being a determinate body is inconceivable for him who remains faithful to Aristotle. We must conclude that for St. Bonaventure the form has two functions: first, that of giving a certain determination to matter; second, that of preparing matter and rendering it capable of receiving a more perfect form.

With these notions we are now in a position to understand what thoughts and conceptions are at the basis of the famous doctrine of the plurality of forms which characterizes the cosmology of the Augustinian school. It is clear that if there are some forms which do not satisfy the capacity for perfection which is in matter and, in actualizing it, dispose matter to receive a more perfect form, it is not only not repugnant, but rather it is necessary to think that a thing attains its perfect actuality through the subordinate—and not only successive—action of two or more forms. Bodies, to bring ourselves to the concrete, are informed by at least two forms: a general form which makes them to be bodies (it is the form which actuated the matter of the world in the first instant of creation) and another form which makes them to be a certain kind of body: iron, copper, calcium, and so forth.

It is easy to see the application which this doctrine can have in resolving the problem of the fate of the forms of simple bodies when the latter enter into chemical composition as well as its further application with regard to the problem of the relationship between the body and soul in man. If, then, we desire to investigate more deeply into the nature of that first incomplete form with which matter was concretized, we shall find elements sufficient to satisfy our curiosity in St. Bonaventure.

Let us turn our attention to the empyrean heaven created together with matter as the *first* of all the active substances of the corporeal world. The activity of a being is in a direct relationship with the perfection of its form. If, then, the empyrean is the *first* of the active material substances (*first,* evidently, not only in the order of time, but also in the order of nature) and, therefore, the most active of all, one can say that it possesses the most perfect of corporeal forms. The empyrean heaven thus becomes qualified in the plan of creation to assume a function opposed and, at the same time, complementary to that of matter: as matter offers itself as the passive principle of all bodies, so the empyrean heaven presides over, so to speak, and promotes the distribution of all the other forms or active principles.

St. Bonaventure, allying himself here to the physical doctrine taught by Robert Grosseteste and Roger Bacon, believes this most perfect corporeal form which is the original principle of all the other corporeal forms to be light. In outline form the Bonaventurian doctrine of light can be summarized in the following points: light is not an accidental form, as is commonly believed; it is a substantial form. By its nature light is diffusive and instantaneously spreads itself; it invests and empowers matter, so to speak, rendering it capable, by its information, of receiving all the other forms.[2] It is, therefore, a general form of bodies

----

[2] "Forma enim lucis cum ponitur in eodem corpore cum alia forma, non ponitur sicut dispositio imperfecta quae nata sit perfici per ultimam formam, sed ponitur tanquam forma et natura omnis alterius formae corporalis conservativa et dans ei agendi efficaciam, et secundum quam attenditur cuiuslibet formae corporalis mensura in dignitate et excellentia." *In II Sent.,* d. 13, a. 2, q. 2, ad. 5; *Opera*

which is not specified by other forms, as the genus is determined by the specific difference (and hence it is not a universal form in the technical sense of the word); it is the intermediary between matter and form, to which it gives and conserves activity and of which light is the general principle. One understands, then, that a form is so much the more perfect in proportion to the quantity of light which acts in the body. As a form, it is not directly perceived by the senses; nevertheless, it manifests itself through the splendor or color which it communicates to the body.[3]

After these considerations it is not difficult to understand that the empyrean heaven, in which light as its proper substantial form is found in all its purity and efficacy, informs matter from the very moment of its creation and confers on it the aptitude—still undifferentiated—to receive all the corporeal forms. With this aptitude matter receives its primordial information sufficient to give it that physical reality which constitutes it as something extended. Indeed, extension or quantity is the fundamental attribute of corporeal matter as such, before it becomes this or that body. After this beginning, the collaboration between matter—the principle of passivity—and light —the principle of activity—will continue to develop until bodies are completely constituted in all their variety.

It is clear then that, with the creation of the empyrean and matter, God posited the premises of

Omnia, t. II, p. 321.

[3] "Lux non sentitur ratione suae essentiae, sed ratione fulgoris vel coloris eam inseparabiliter concomitantis." *Ibid,* ad. 2.

the whole corporeal world: premises which, however, would always have remained such without the successive creative interventions of God which were necessary to guide and to actualize the unfolding of mundane reality in all its variety and magnificence. This development was only potentially contained in the two first principles studied.

Another characteristic theme of Augustinian cosmology in general and Bonaventurian cosmology in particular is that of the "rationes seminales." The problem which this doctrine proposes to answer can be formulated in this fashion: it is a fact of daily experience that creation in some manner continues. New beings appear before our eyes at every moment, whether through generation or chemical composition. From hydrogen and oxygen, as often as I wish, I can produce water which is a new reality with a nature and characteristics completely different from those of the simple elements which comprise it. The animals of every species in their turn generate an immense multitude of their own kind. The term of the generative act as well as that of chemical composition implied for the scholastics the arising of a new substantial form, necessary to constitute the new being in its natural concreteness. Are these new forms which arise through the action of a created agent drawn from nothing, or do they already pre-exist in the heart of matter? This, in its widest formulation, is the problem which St. Bonaventure wishes to resolve with his doctrine of the "rationes seminales."

Ingenious solutions had already been proposed by the ancients and the contemporaries of the Seraphic Doctor but they did not satisfy the demands of his spirit, preoccupied, on the one hand, with reserving to God alone the efficacy and perfection of the creative act and, on the other hand, with safeguarding the causality of the creature. According to the opinion attributed to Anaxagoras, all the forms which appear by degrees in the world pre-exist distinctly in matter. They are not evident only because their operations are impeded by a covering which hides them. The action of the agents that intervene in the production of a new body is reduced to placing the necessary conditions in which the new form may be manifested. Others think that the forms which appear are drawn from nothingness by a creative act of God. Created agents produce nothing. By their action they merely offer the occasion for the intervention of the creative act by preparing the matter for the new form. Both opinions are unacceptable to St. Bonaventure because they minimize too much the action of the agents, denying to them a direct causality with regard to the new forms produced. Their action remains extrinsic and it is only by an abuse of language that it can be said that one thing produces another.

The two views mentioned above, however, can be interpreted in a correct sense by saying with the first that the forms pre-exist *virtually* in matter, and with the second that God is the principal efficient cause in the production of new beings. This appears to the Seraphic Doctor to have been the opinion of Aristotle and it merits his approval. The word "virtually," however, can be understood in two ways. Some reduce this virtuality to the receptive capacity of matter in regard to the forms. In receiving them, matter cooperates with the created agent in their production—the result of the passive causality of matter and the active causality of the agents which in their own form find the power to transmit it and to multiply it in other beings. This is the position defended by St. Thomas.

To St. Bonaventure this solution seems to concede too much to the action of the created agent. To say that a production of forms as described above is not a creation because the forms are not drawn from nothing but from matter and the agent—realities already existing—is not sufficiently cogent for the Seraphic Doctor. Actually, the new form is produced exclusively by the agent; matter has only a receptive function. Rather than an eduction of the forms from matter, it should be said to be a creation of the forms in matter. For this reason St. Bonaventure proposes another solution elaborated in the Augustinian doctrine of the "rationes seminales."

The forms pre-exist in matter not only because matter can and, in a certain sense, longs to receive them, but because there is concreated in matter a "quid," essentially distinct from it, from which the action of the agent draws the new form. This "quid" is not a part of the future form but something which can become that given form. It is the form in the state of potency which will be reduced to act by the agent which produces it. These agents do not give it a new "quidditas"; they merely produce a new *disposition* in it by which it passes from the state of potentiality to that of actuality. The act does not bring about a new essential entity to that which was in potency, but it changes the dispositions of it or its manner of being; thus producing in it a change which, although it is not of the essential order, is nevertheless of the substantial order. Certainly no one would admit that between being in potency and being in act there is only an accidental difference. This solution has the advantage of according to the agent a direct and intrinsic action on the form produced inasmuch as through its activity there results a new manner of being. The first two opinions attribute to the agent merely an indirect and extrinsic activity with regard to the production of the actual form. It does not, however, concede to the agent—as the third opinion does—the production of a new essential entity which is most difficult to understand without a creative act.

To that "quid" concreated in matter from which the agent educes the new form in the sense explained, St. Bonaventure gives the name "ratio seminalis" which was coined by St. Augustine. Gilson[4] proposes this definition of it: "the 'ratio seminalis' is the essence of the form considered under the mode of incomplete being." Matter, then, concurs in the production of new beings not only passively but also actively by means of the 'rationes seminales,' which are, as it were, the active powers of matter.

Having established the existence and nature of the

---

[4] *La Philosophie* . . ., p. 291. This definition is derived from the following text of St. Bonaventure: "Ad praedictorum intelligentiam est notandum, quod cum satis constet rationem seminalem, esse potentiam activam, inditam materiae; et illam potentiam activam constet esse essentiam formae, cum ex ea fiat forma mediate operatione naturae, quae non producit aliquid ex nihilo: satis rationabiliter ponitur, quod ratio seminalis est essentia formae producendae; differens ab illa, secundum esse in potentia et in actu." *In II Sent.*, d. 18, a. I, q. 3; *Opera Omnia*, t. II, p. 440.

"rationes," a further question remains to be resolved. Their incompleteness places in them a certain indetermination because of which many particular beings find their root in the "rationes." Some exaggerated realists have drawn away from this indetermination of the "rationes" in order to identify them with the Platonic universal forms, existing, however, in the bosom of matter. The universals, indeed, as the "rationes," are in act with respect to matter and in potency with respect to the form of the beings of concrete reality and, therefore, represent, as it were, a bridge between the two principles which renders their fruitful encounter more facile and comprehensible.

St. Bonaventure does not accept this identification. The process of determination which goes from the universal to the particular develops on a metaphysical and logical plane; the process of determination which goes from the "ratio seminalis" to the complete form develops on a physical plane. To confuse the two or to directly identify them would lead to inadmissible consequences, one of which would be that the indetermination of the universal would be taken away by the coming about of a new form which can only be an individual form. It must not be forgotten that the "rationes seminales" are destined to explain the production of new beings. This production, in order that it be effective, must have as its term something substantial. If, therefore, the "ratio seminalis" were the universal form of the thing produced, the term of the productive act could only be a particular substantial form which would take away the incompleteness and indetermination of the universal form, realizing it as individual. This theory would be admissible only for him who holds that the principle of individuation is on the part of the form. This is not admitted by the Seraphic Doctor according to whom individuation arises only from the encounter of matter with the form. Moreover, if this opinion were true, the enrichment which the natural agent introduces into the "ratio seminalis" would be of the essential order and would hence import the creation of a new entity. This is absolutely excluded by St. Bonaventure.

The indetermination or universality of the "ratio seminalis" must be understood in a different way: "radicaliter," says the Seraphic Doctor. It is as the indetermination of a seed or of a force which can produce many effects; that certain indifference a principle has from which many things take their origin. The natural agent which produces the new being takes away this indetermination by communicating to the "ratio seminalis" a part of that store or reserve of activity contained in its own form, thus determining it to pass from potency to act. The "ratio seminalis" not only begins the life or development of a form, but it also closes it. Corporeal forms, after they have exhausted the sum of the energy which they have carried and thus have brought about the death of the being they have constituted in union with matter, return anew to the potential state proper to the "rationes seminales."[5]

Before closing this chapter I would like to point out to the reader, if he has not already noticed it himself,

---

[5] "Ad illud stat resolutio a quo incipit generatio: ergo nulla forma omnino corrumpitur, sed manet in materia post corruptionem, sicut manebat antequam produceretur." *In IV Sent.*, d. 43, a. I, q. 4; *Opera Omnia*, t. IV, p. 888.

an important observation. The cosmological theses of St. Bonaventure, notwithstanding their mediaeval setting, give us a dynamic conception of reality which has a distinctly modern flavor. The Aristotelian conception of matter which tends to embrace the form as its act and its perfection also places in the very heart of things a metaphysical dynamism of notable significance. This dynamism, however, is much more accentuated in St. Bonaventure. His doctrine on the unformed physical matter in the bosom of which the "rationes seminales" are in ferment under the influence of light, the perfect vivifying and promoting form of activity, places in the heart of all reality a metaphysical impulse toward being and perfection unknown to Aristotelianism. The doctrine of the plurality of forms, which mark, so to speak, the stages of this journey of things toward being, ends with rendering almost perceptible and evident the interior travail of reality, in which doctrine there is found the explanation for the immense hierarchy of beings which compose the world, and the ordered discipline with which the imperfect being is sacrificed, one might say, in order to nourish the life of the more perfect.

MAN: HIS NATURE AND ACTIVITY

Man occupies a central place in the plan of creation. In him the spiritual and corporal natures meet and are bound together in a magnificent synthesis mysterious to us in so many ways. In his body the vast and complex laws of corporeal nature unite forces to produce their most representative and most perfect fruit; while in his soul—not inferior by nature to the angels but united substantially to the body— the spirit descends to lift up the material world to the destiny of the spiritual. Man thus becomes the natural mediator between creation and God, blending together in himself the voices of the whole universe. Capable of God by his intelligence and his love, man leads the world back to its Supreme Maker. With this we have already given the most noble reason for man's creation; and at the same time we perceive the interest and the promise with which man claims the attention of every thinker and St. Bonaventure in particular, who, preoccupied as he was with the Neo-Platonic good, sought to find the link which would rejoin multiplicity to unity. The greatest problem of psychology is that of discovering the nature of the union between soul and body.

Philosophical tradition offered two opposing solutions to the consideration of St. Bonaventure: that of Plato and Aristotle. St. Augustine, however, had

already perceived that Plato could very well be reconciled with Aristotle in a third solution which would
save with the first the metaphysical independence of
the soul with regard to the body, and with the second
the fact that their union is not violent but natural.
St. Bonaventure follows substantially the path of St.
Augustine. The formula which he uses to characterize the manner of the union between the body
and the soul is Aristotelian: the soul for St.
Bonaventure also is the form of the body. But as
usual under an identity of formulas there lies hidden
a profound difference of conceptions.

Let us begin by recalling that for the Seraphic
Doctor the soul, as all spiritual natures, is already
itself composed of matter and form. This matter, of
course, is not corporeal or physical; it is matter understood as the metaphysical principle of all being which
in some manner is in potency and becoming. One
immediately realizes that the soul is not merely a form,
that is, a something which can exist only as a coprinciple of being together with matter; if it is a form with
regard to the body, nevertheless being a form does not
constitute its total reality.[1] Although the soul presents
itself to our observation as that which causes man to
exist in his corporeal concreteness and is the source
of his life, perception and understanding, nevertheless
the soul is first of all a spiritual substance and hence
a being which can exist by itself and in its own right.
The arguments which constrain us to admit the
spirituality of the soul also oblige us to conclude that

---

[1] ". . . Non tantum forma est, verum etiam hoc aliquid." *Breviloquium*, pars II, *c*. 9; *Opera Omnia*, t.
V. p. 227.

it is a spiritual substance—a being, "hoc aliquid"—
and not only a coprinciple of being in the sense of any
form whatsoever understood in its precise metaphysical meaning.

The divergence from Aristotle increases. He who
wishes to follow the pure lines of Aristotelian thought
cannot admit that a substance, in uniting itself with
another thing, gives rise to a substantial composite.
Only if two realities are exclusively in a relationship
of matter and form can they give rise to a substantial unity. If the soul is already a substance on its own
account, the union with the body, in whatever manner it is conceived, will always be accidental—unless
one accepts the doctrine of the plurality of forms.
This is the case with St. Bonaventure. And it is precisely in recurring to those considerations which lie
at the basis of such a doctrine that one solves the
difficulty which can be advanced by a follower of
Aristotle.

The statement that there cannot be substantial
composition among beings already complete in themselves—observes the Seraphic Doctor—is not true in
all cases. It is true only when the form completely ex-
hausts the potentiality of the matter and the matter
completely absorbs the activity of the form. In his
case the possibilities of the one are completely actuated by the perfective act of the other, and reciprocal-
ly the form has completely realized its efficacy in the
matter. Their encounter, therefore, has produced in
them a metaphysical satiety which excludes any further appetite. It removes any possibility of another
thing being joined to the resulting substance in an
essential union. This is not the case in regard to the
soul and the body. For, on the one hand, the rational

soul tends by a natural inclination to become the perfective act of the corporeal nature; and the human
body, on the other hand, inasmuch as it is already
composed of matter and form, inclines with a metaphysical desire toward the soul as to its further perfection. Neither has the form of the soul diffused
all its realizable power in the spiritual matter, nor has
the form of the body exhausted the capacity of its
matter. The human body is the final stage of that
metaphysical dynamism which the promoting influence of light stirs up and maintains in the corporeal
matter, drawing the sensible nature from perfection
to perfection. This dynamism encounters that of the
spiritual substance and together they tend to attract
everything in their intelligent and loving impulse
toward God as the supreme Good and final cause of
all creation.[2] The union, then, between the soul and
body in man is natural and corresponds to a recipro-
cal inclination of an essential order. How can it be
said that the composition which results is only accidental?

In this conception the relationships between the
soul and the body are profoundly different from those

---

[2] ". . . Corpora humana . . . disposita sunt ad nobilis-
simam formam, quae est anima rationalis; ad quam
ordinatur et terminatur appetitu omnis naturae sens-
ibilis et corporalis, ut per eam quae est forma, ens,
vivens, sentiens et intelligens, quasi ad modum cir-
culi intelligibilis reducatur ad suum principium; in
quo perficiatur et beatificetur." *Ibid.,* c. 4; *Opera
Omnia,* t. V. p. 221. This is an idea dear to St.
Bonaventure and is expressed in numerous passages
of his works; e.g., *In II Sent.,* d. 17, a. I, q. 3, concl.
et ad 4; *ibid.,* t. II, p. 417; d. 18, a. 2, q. 2, concl.
et ad 2; *ibid.,* p. 449.

which would cause one to suspect the formula which
St. Bonaventure uses in common with Aristotelianism.
The human soul is not form which seeks in the body
its ontological wholeness in the order of being and
acting. It is a form which is united to matter in
order to share with it the perfection which it has in
its own right; a form which lowers itself in order to
ennoble matter. At the same time the Platonic conception is profoundly correct. One can certainly say
in the precise sense of the word that the soul *descends*
into the body. But since the soul is by its very nature
destined for the body and naturally ordered to it, its
union with the body is neither violent nor debasing.
Rather it represents a perfection for the soul. In contradistinction to the separated spiritual substances,
the human soul, through its union with the body,
sums up in itself the aspirations of all created nature
and thus becomes the most noble of all forms. The
difference, on the other hand, between Plato and St.
Bonaventure is found clearly stated in these words:
"Although the soul is said to be united to the human
body or enlivens the human body, nevertheless, it
is not an accidental or ignoble act. It is not an accidental act because by its very nature the soul is a substantial form. It is not an ignoble act because by its
very nature the soul is the most noble of all forms
and in the soul is found the longing of all creation."[3]

---

[3] "Hoc enim, quod est animam uniri corpori humano
sive vivificare corpus humanum, non dicit actum
accidentalem nec dicit actum ignobilem: non *accidentalem,* quia ratione illius est forma substantialis;
non *ignobilem,* quia ratione illius est anima nobilis-
sima formarum omnium, et in anima stat appetitus

Another important consequence derives from the admission that the soul is composed of matter and form: the individuation of the soul does not depend on its union with the body. It comes from the soul itself. All Christian thought maintains that personality is the most valuable gift that man possesses. If this is true, one immediately sees the incongruity of making this ultimate and highest perfection of the spirit depend on its union with the body. This is particularly repugnant to him who, along with St. Bonaventure, conceives the soul as a substance complete in itself. It is to be expected that non-Christian thinkers such as Aristotle and Averroes should have conceived it thus. For them the individual, inasmuch as it is the ultimate realization of the species, is of less value than the species itself. The succession of individuals has as its fundamental purpose the perpetuation of the species. But if things, and especially man, have been created in order to manifest the divine goodness, the multiplicity of individuals finds its explanation in the possibility and suitability of granting to other beings participation in the banquet of the inexhaustible divine munificence—and this in thousands of ways and in most varied degrees. With this we have taken away the foundation of the Averroistic doctrine of the unity of the agent intellect. Averroes based his main arguments on the fact that the soul is individuated only by its union with the body.

It is, moreover, easily observed that in the light of the Bonaventurian conception the demonstration

totius naturae." *In II Sent.*, d. 1, pars II, a. 3, q. 2; *Opera Omnia*, t. II, p. 50.

of the immortality of the soul proceeds, one might say, without encountering serious obstacles. The subsistence of the separated soul is most comprehensible, although it continually aspires to reunion with the body through that natural appetite which binds it vitally to the body. It is not its union with the body, as Plato thought, but its separation from the body which is violent. St. Bonaventure gathers together the numerous traditional arguments in order to demonstrate the immortality of the soul. In treating of a fundamental truth almost as basic as the existence of God, it is useful to set forth the different points of view and to multiply the reasons which convince us of it.

For the Seraphic Doctor, however, there is only one conclusive argument: man could not attain the end for which he has been created without immortality. Brought from nothing in order to close the circle of creation which without him could not have been reunited to God, the end of man is precisely that of adhering to Him with his intelligence and his will. Man certainly does not attain his end in this world, where our knowledge of God is so vague, distant, difficult and indirect; our will, so distracted and weak. Even though we seek God with that persevering strength and ardent desire which can lead us at most to the peace of contemplation of the beatifying light of ecstasy, nevertheless to possess Him fully, to satisfy our capacity for Him perfectly and eternally is not possible in this life. Only immortality will allow us to take the decisive step toward the final cause of creation and the ultimate object of our understanding and love. Death understood as total destruction is metaphysically repulsive to the human soul. Created to know and to love God, its destiny is bound to its object.

In the *Breviloquium,* a work in which St. Bonaventure proceeds only by the deductive method—the method proper to all Neo-Platonic thought—the Seraphic Doctor places the immortality of the soul at the basis of his whole psychology. And rightly so, if the being and action of everything are measured by the object and end to which they are destined. The soul is not only man's act of existence but also the principle of all his operations through the three faculties—vegetative, sensitive, and rational. This last is composed of intellect and will. As can be seen, St. Bonaventure, in determining the psychological structure of human action, agrees substantially with Aristotle, but not without introducing into the development of the theory original interpretations and patterns of thought which are Augustinian in character. It is in this spirit that he sets in relief and stresses the importance of the sensible and intellectual memory. He never considers it, however, as a faculty distinct from the intellect and the various denominations or classifications of the cognitive faculty which are found at almost every step in the works of the Seraphic Doctor—which he preserves in order to characterize the many functions and the manifold aspects with which our cognitive activity presents itself.

He gives, on the other hand, a personal solution to the problem of the relationship between the soul and its faculties. St. Augustine tended to confuse the faculties with the soul and regarded their separate designations as completely extrinsic in character, having their basis only in the different relations which are established between the soul and the objects to which it is directed. St. Thomas, on the contrary, considers the faculties as true accidents of the soul, which are joined to its essence and really distinct—although inseparable—from it. They are proper accidents or properties of the soul. The opinion of St. Bonaventure mediates between those of St. Augustine and St. Thomas. The faculties are identified with the essence of the soul. They are not sufficiently distinct from its essence to constitute its properties. The faculties are ontologically reduced to the soul inasmuch as they do not have any being distinct from that of its essence. But at the same time they are not merely extrinsic denominations; they are true modes of the soul's action. They emerge from its essence, but without thereby becoming so separated from it as to be able to be called accidents. St. Bonaventure says they are "consubstantiales" with the soul. If we abstract from its faculties, the very essence of the soul, so to speak, disappears; while, on the other hand, this essence is precisely neither the intellect nor the will.

We cannot then speak of a real distinction between the soul and its faculties, but rather of a distinction which resembles that which exists between the divine essence and its attributes. There is also a certain circumincession between the soul and its faculties and the faculties with themselves, in the sense that one recalls the other. We cannot even conceive the soul if we prescind from the intellect and the will, just as we cannot conceive an intellective and volitive act if we prescind from the rationality which is the constitutive element of the soul. This doctrine stands at the foundation of the Bonaventurian conception of sensation.

For St. Augustine sensation is the act by which the

soul knows the exterior agent which has modified our
sense organ. For St. Thomas sensation is the act by
which the composite reaches the concrete sensible
qualities; only indirectly is it an act of the soul,
namely, only insofar as the sensitive faculty is rooted
in the soul. Once again St. Bonaventure's opinion
mediates between the two. Sensation is a passive mod-
ification of the composite. But inasmuch as it is inseparable from the judgment by which we perceive
the object as beautiful, pleasing, beneficial or not, it
must be said that sensation begins in the sense organ
but is completed in the soul. Beauty consists in an
exact numerical relationship; pleasure in a proportion; salubrity in a suitability between the object
and our sense organ. All these things indicate a penetration of rationality into sensation. Thus sensation in
man is quite different from that of every other ani-
mal.

The Augustinian tendency of the Seraphic Doctor's
psychology finds its most important and significant
application in his theory of knowledge. Human
knowledge can be studied from two different points
of view. One can seek to determine its psychological
elements and moments, and then concentrate on understanding how the intellective act comes about and
how concepts are formed in our mind. Or one can
examine the fundamental realities which make our
knowledge possible. In the first case we strive to describe the psychology of knowledge and resolve the
problem of the origin of ideas. In the second case we
attempt to delineate the metaphysical structure of
human knowing and resolve the problem of the
value of our concepts. Aristotelianism is above all a
psychology. Platonism, on the other hand, is first

of all a metaphysics of knowledge. St. Bonaventure strove to take both aspects into account, and his theory of knowledge is an attempt to integrate the one doctrine with the other.

The Aristotelian theory of knowledge is essentially a theory of abstraction. And it is with abstraction that St. Bonaventure also begins. The objects which first affect our intellect are the things of our external experience with which sensation places us in contact. This is our first manner of knowing them. The knowledge which we gain of sensible things is completely an acquiring; our mind is a "tabula rasa" in regard to them. From our first encounter with things by means of sensation, to the formation of corresponding concepts by means of the intellective act, a psychological process is at work. St. Bonaventure makes his own the analysis which Aristotle had made of it, and he resolves this process into the same elements: sensation, the phantasm, the agent intellect, the "species intelligibilis," and the possible intellect.

With regard to the agent and possible intellect, however, a significant observation must be made, the importance of which we shall understand later on. The Seraphic Doctor points out that the denominations "*agent* intellect" and "*possible* intellect" are not to be taken too rigorously; neither is the first completely lacking in passivity nor is the second deprived of all initiative. The agent intellect does not work alone in the formation of the concept but requires the collaboration of the "species" on which it depends in its action. The possible intellect, on the other hand, turns on its own initiative to the phantasm and once the "species intelligibilis" is formed by means of the action of the agent intellect, the possible intellect receives the "species," but not in a completely passive manner. For in receiving the "species," the possible intellect forms a judgment concerning it. As I have said, we shall understand the value of these remarks later; for now we shall move on.

We know not only sensible things, the objects of our external experience, but we also have knowledge of the soul and God. And with regard to the soul and God one can certainly not speak of abstraction. Knowledge comes about through an assimilation of the object on the part of the subject; and abstraction is precisely this process by which we assimilate sensible things into our spiritual soul, stripping them of their material condition. This process of purification is clearly not necessary when it is a question of knowing our soul, its qualities and powers. Nothing is more like a thing than the thing itself; and if the intellect which knows is not identical with the essence of the soul, it is nevertheless consubstantial with it.

The case of God is even clearer. If we know Him, it is certainly not because we assimilate Him to ourselves through some kind of abstraction, but because He places in us a likeness—a "similitudo"—of Himself. It is impossible, therefore, to affirm with Aristotle that all knowledge comes to us from the senses. We must admit that there is another source from which we derive our concepts of spiritual things in general and of God in particular.

The knowledge, moreover, which comes to us from sensible things is organized according to necessary laws which we call first principles. It is true that we formulate these principles on the occasion of experience; but it is also just as true that their value transcends experience, and they are valid even when we reflect on God and on merely possible things. Man, who is a mutable being, surrounded by and in contact only with unstable, contingent and precarious things, succeeds in gaining from these things a knowledge which is immutable, necessary and infallible. We are in the midst of a continuous change of impressions, of experiences, and of scientific, historical and philosophical hypotheses, causing man to despair of arriving at the truth which, of its nature, is immutable and eternal. And yet it is an undeniable fact that, in this tumult, unshakeable certitudes rise up as reefs jutting out of a boiling sea. But lest the comparison with reefs mislead us, we must speak rather of ideal laws which cross, as lines of eternal force, all of the uncertain and the mutable in our cognition and give them value, organization and unity. They compose the spontaneous and at the same time necessary network of human knowing from which no mind can escape.

These ideal laws which we find within ourselves are the norms and rules according to which we judge all things including our soul and its reflections. If, then, our mind is subject to them and they are the basic criteria by which we judge even ourselves, one can say that although we find them in our soul as part of its native endowment, they do not thereby proceed from it but have been given to it by an agent superior to the soul. They have been given by God, affirms St. Bonaventure. Who, indeed, knows mutable, contingent and temporal things in an infallible, eternal and immutable manner if not God

Who knows all things in the "rationes aeternae"?[4]
If, therefore, we know things not only as they are, but
even as they must be, we can say that our mind also
knows them in their "rationes aeternae." This is the
expression which St. Bonaventure uses to characterize
that doctrine which is usually called "the theory of
intellectual illumination," a doctrine which is found
with widely different interpretations in all the thinkers who accept Platonic-Augustinian epistemology.

Having seen—with the brevity inevitably imposed
by the nature of this profile—those considerations
which led St. Bonaventure to affirm the necessity and
the existence of intellectual illumination, we are now
constrained to state with precision its mechanism and
its elements. The reader is now in the position to understand what the "rationes aeternae" are: they are
the eternal archetypes of all possible things, which
God eternally expresses in the word or the divine idea,
through which God knows perfectly every being
created and creatable. We note here that these "rationes aeternae," precisely because they are divine
ideas, are not only means by which God knows things;
they have a normative efficacy in things according

---

[4] Do not confuse the problem which St. Bonaventure
here proposes with the problem concerning the ontological foundation of truth. St. Bonaventure is not
asking what is the being which guarantees the existence of eternal and immutable truth, but rather
*how can one explain the presence of necessary,
immutable and unshakeable truths in the mind of
man.* His is not a problem of general metaphysics,
but of epistemology or, to be more explicit, a problem which enters into every metaphysical inquiry
of human thought.

to which things are patterned in regard to both their existence and their perfection. This active aspect of the "ratio aeterna" in relation to the thing is very clearly brought out by St. Bonaventure. Another expression which he uses when speaking of the "ratio aeterna" is the "similitudo exemplativa," that is, a pattern which directly forms or molds its copies.

To know a being, therefore, in its "ratio aeterna" is to know it not only as it is actually but also as it must be; to know it in its eternal and necessary roots and not only as it is offered to us by experience. If the only source of our knowledge was the being with which things are presented to us, we would not succeed in rising to the concept and to science, and our knowledge would be an apprehension without judgment. If we are rescued from the plane of contingency and becoming on which we and things are found, it is only in virtue of the "rationes aeternae" which our mind "aliquo modo" attains. The difficulty with the theory lies in determining as far as possible the meaning of "aliquo modo."

The "ratio aeterna" is not the "tota et sola" cause of our knowledge. If it were, our knowledge would be identical with that of God Who knows all things in the word inasmuch as it is the adequate expression of the divine essence and all the possibles. The existence or the presence of created things would have no influence on our intellect, just as it in no way influences God's understanding; a state of affairs which is absurd and contradicted by experience. The "ratio aeterna" does not determine intrinsically; it is not the formal cause of our intellective act. It does, however, efficaciously aid every step of our knowledge as a superior norm, as a force which impels us from knowledge to knowledge until we arrive at the supreme unification of all reality. It is the norm with its evidence which is imposed on our mind and which carries us with logical necessity toward the ultimate causes because of which reality is and appears rational to us.[5] Our knowledge is thus revealed to us as sustained by God and more precisely by knowing God, in view of the fact that the "rationes aeternae" are divine ideas. It remains, therefore, to resolve the problem of how our thought is nourished by the thought of God or, putting aside all metaphor, how intellectual illumination comes about.

Excluding the possibility that our knowledge is identified with that of God, which would be equivalent to saying that God knows in us, a necessary point of contact must be found between our mind and God. The presence of the "ratio aeterna" in our mind would be useless and inefficacious if we did not have some cognition of it. In order to act on our thought it is necessary that God in some manner communicate Himself to our thought—a communication which must be not only of the ontological but also of the intellectual order.[6] But how precisely is this "influence" of which St. Bonaventure speaks realized? What effect does it produce in our soul? The effect can only be the impression of a certain knowledge of God in us by means of a "similitudo" or "species Dei" which enables us to know Him. For we cannot know God except insofar as He likens us to Himself

---

[5] St. Bonaventure expresses this fact when he says that the "ratio aeterna" is "regulans et motiva."

[6] "Non solum requiritur lucis aeternae praesentia, sed etiam lucis aeternae influentia." *De scientia Christi*, q. 7, epilogus; *Opera Omnia*, t. V, p. 42.

by impressing in us an idea of His divine essence which is proportionate to our actual capacity. Making us capable of knowing God, this innate idea enables us at the same time to know all other things. As only God is being in the full sense of the word, so also He alone is Perfect Truth; and as our being exists only inasmuch as it is analogous to the divine knowledge.

The "similitudo" or idea of God which is impressed in us and raises our soul to the dignity of His image tends to repeat in our intellect the same order of knowing which is proper to the divine intellect and which, as such, constitutes the model and the necessary rule of all knowing. God in knowing His essence knows all things in it. We, naturally incapable of an intuition of God and hence of knowing all things in Him, must turn to experience and reasoning in order to acquire our cognition of things; but every movement of our intellect will be made in virtue of that innate idea of God which is the light and the rule of all knowing. The essence of our knowledge, which is precisely that of being a living analogy of divine knowledge as all things are vibrant analogies of God's being, is constituted by this "species Dei" impressed in our soul. It is this which renders our thinking possible and is actually the beginning of it in imitation of the divine thought.

From this idea of the Supreme Being arise the concepts of unity, goodness and truth, and with that the theoretical and practical first principles. The soul is thus equipped with all that it requires to arrive at the truth: with the idea of the Supreme Being it has grasped implicitly the laws or formal schemas of rationality which will develop and become conscious to us from our contact with experience. Although the soul does not know all things, nevertheless, it is placed in the condition to know and judge all things.

The necessity of our turning to experience, not only to have a distinct and proper knowledge of things but also to develop and determine the very idea which we have of God and the system of rationality, is strongly affirmed by St. Bonaventure. It can, however, be asked of us whether experience merely provides the occasion for the development of knowledge within us or, on the other hand, if experience produces it as its efficient cause. There is no doubt of where the Seraphic Doctor stands on this point, and he takes his position not only because he condemns Platonic epistemology and affirms with Aristotle that our soul is initially a "tabula rasa" with regard to things, but also because the very logic of his thought demands it.

In order to know things in God it would be necessary that the idea which we have of Him be adequate and perfect; actually it is only a confused and inadequate idea. But if we do not even know God clearly, much less will it be possible to know other things distinctly in Him. In order to arrive at a proper and distinct knowledge of things, it is necessary that they themselves come in contact with us and add the light or truth which they carry in themselves to the light which our intellect derives from the idea born of God. Experience, therefore, is a true and proper source of our knowledge of sensible things. But in regard to our knowledge of spiritual substances, of God and the first principles, experience is only the occasion by which our mind passes from an implicit to an explicit knowledge.

To conclude, then, the intellectual illumination of St. Bonaventure requires the extrinsic assistance of God in the intellectual order which is given to our mind with the impression of the idea of God. The idea by which God knows Himself produces eternally and necessarily the "rationes aeternae" of things. In like manner the idea of God innate in our soul produces necessarily the theoretical and practical first principles and all the laws of rationality. They invest and unify our knowledge gradually acquired through experience, giving to it the characteristics of necessity, immutability and absoluteness which are proper to truth.

I shall close this concise exposition of the Bonaventurian theory of illumination[7]—a theory which although it is common to all the Augustinians is well-known but rarely understood—with some opportune observations. One cannot speak of ontologism in St. Bonaventure unless he clearly distinguishes in what sense he is using the term. Actually, the knowledge of God which the Seraphic Doctor attributes to man is neither more perfect nor more profound than that which St. Thomas and every other Christian thinker admits. Even for St. Bonaventure one cannot speak of an intuition and much less of a vision of God "sicut est." This doctrine, as it is taught in the manuals of systematic philosophy, would be essential to an ontologistic epistemology, as well as the logical consequence which derives from it: that man knows

[7] If the reader wishes to learn more on this point of Bonaventurian doctrine, I refer him to the following article: "La dottrina bonaventuriana dell' illuminazione intellettuale," *"Rivista di filosofia neoscolastica,"* 1944, t. XXXVI, pp. 139-158.

all things in God. We have carefully stressed the imperfection of the knowledge of God actually possible
to man and the necessity of experience for our intellect to pass from potency to act. St. Bonaventure,
however, differs from St. Thomas in that he considers
God not only the point of arrival for human thought
but also its point of departure. He maintains further
that without this point of departure we could never
achieve the goal of our knowing—the knowledge of
God. Indeed, even knowledge in general would be
impossible for us. Not content with describing the
"itinerarium" of our mind to God, St. Bonaventure
also teaches us what the foundation is that renders
possible the existence itself, as well as the accomplish-
ment of the "itinerarium." For the Seraphic Doctor
this foundation or basis is the innate idea of God.
Here we have the difference between the five ways
of St. Thomas and the innumerable considerations
with which the Seraphic Doctor establishes the existence of God.

The objections which are usually brought against
innatism (e.g., Locke's criticism of Cartesian innatism) do not avail against Bonaventurian innatism.
We have not said that we have a finely formed, clear
and complete idea of God, but only the elements
with which to elaborate it; and we are not conscious
even of these. The term "innate" for St. Bonaventure means only this: that there is given an idea
which is not derived by abstraction from sensible
things, but is formed by an elaboration or development which is completely interior to the soul, although only in contact with and on the occasion of
experience. The innatism of St. Bonaventure is a

dynamic innatism and not a static one against which the above-mentioned objections are advanced.

The discerning reader cannot avoid seeing a certain analogy between St. Bonaventure and Kant. For both rationality and its laws are within us: we apply them to experience, we do not derive them therefrom. The similarity, however, ends here. For Kant the "a priori" has its absolute foundation in the creativity of our spirit understood not as the empirical "I" but as the transcendental "I." For St. Bonaventure the "a priori" is merely a human participation in the divine thought which has created things according to the archetypes eternally generated with and in the word. Kant ends in absolute subjectivity while St. Bonaventure guarantees the objectivity of our thought by basing it on the absolute objectivity of divine knowledge. And thus the abyss between the two thinkers remains intact: the abyss between immanence and transcendence.

We can make a perfect parallel between matter and our intellect at the moment of their creation. Matter receives its first information—sufficient to make it exist but not to determine it—from the light of the empyrean heaven which renders it capable of receiving all the other corporeal forms. The function of light, however, does not stop here. By its influence it promotes and makes fruitful all of the successive informations of matter until the most perfect is arrived at: the union between the body and soul in man. God, Whom St. Bonaventure so often calls "uncreated light," has the same function with regard to our intellect as light has in regard to matter. By impressing His image—this innate idea—on our soul, He causes it to exist as intellect, leaving it undetermined, however, with regard to all of the particular or determined ideas of things. Although this idea gives us the possession of no determinate knowledge, it nevertheless renders us capable of knowing all things by assisting, promoting and regulating our every step toward truth.

Our intellect, then, as matter, is never without act. In the beginning its act is most imperfect, but it is only in virtue of that first act that we are capable of all the other acts which form the perfection of our intellect. While we note that the doctrine of the plurality of forms helps us to understand the Bonaventurian theory of knowledge, we must observe that the possible intellect of St. Bonaventure is neither the possible intellect of Aristotle nor of St. Thomas. It is "quodammodo materia prima," but "quodammodo" physical—not metaphysical—matter; and therefore it is not pure passivity. The most imperfect actuality which it possesses, inasmuch as it is informed by the idea of God, renders it not only capable but desirous of knowing. It is the possible intellect which turns to the phantasm of a thing in order to render it intelligible and which solicits the collaboration of the agent intellect. It is, furthermore, the possible intellect which seals the intellective act by judging rather than by receiving the object present in the "species intelligibilis" and assigning to it its place in the system of rationality. The Aristotelian distinction between the agent intellect and the possible intellect thus loses much of its importance. Actually, for St. Bonaventure they are only two different moments of the activity which our intellect displays, when, in order to know a sensible being, it must follow the way of abstraction. Naturally the

root of the activity of the agent intellect, as that
of the possible, is one: the fruitful assistance of the
uncreated light—the source of all intellectual dynamism.

ITINERARIUM MENTIS IN DEUM

Exemplarism explains the emanation of things from God; illumination the return of the multiple to unity. This return is accomplished in two stages: in the first, creation, through that metaphysical rhythm of reality whose principal laws we have seen, beginning with unformed matter, arrives through infinite grades at the constitution of man; in the second, through the intelligence and will of man, creation becomes a mirror of the divine perfections and a poem not of words but of real things which exalts the goodness and the glory of God and prepares man for union with God first through ecstasy and then the Beatific Vision. To describe what the conditions and moments of this second phase are which must overflow from the depths of the human soul into all of man's works and inspire his culture and civilization is the matter of that Bonaventurian work entitled *Itinerarium mentis in Deum*. I shall attempt here with a few sober observations to place in relief the substantial lines of this treatise.

Through illumination man becomes the image of God and God the object, the final end of the human understanding and will. Parallel and analogous to intellectual illumination is moral illumination, which makes the will capable of directing itself toward God and uniting itself to Him. Not only do the theoretical first principles proceed from the idea of God innate in man's soul, but also the practical first principles which constitute conscience, the supreme norm of our conduct. Conscience, however, although it directs our will, does not intrinsically determine it. It is a part of the intellective faculty which is both speculative and practical.

Divine illumination directly affects the will by impressing in it a natural—and hence indestructible—inclination toward the good. It is a power or weight which directs the will not to the good in so far as it is suitable, pleasing and useful, but to the good for its own sake. This inclination, which St. Bonaventure calls "synderesis," has the same function and the same efficacy with regard to the will as the innate idea has with regard to the intellect. It constitutes the will as rational, making God its object and thus becoming the nourishing source of all our affections and all our desires. It is "synderesis" which makes us aware of the fact that the goods which we gradually acquire are not the supreme good, the true good, which we must seek more diligently. As the innate idea of God tends to repeat in us the order of divine knowing, so this natural inclination tends to repeat in our will the order of God's love, through which He loves Himself as the only True Good and creatures only in so far as they are reflections or living likenesses of His fontal goodness. God is not only the exemplary cause of things but also of action and of virtue, which are nothing else but modes of the perfect activity. St. Bonaventure reduces all the virtues to the four cardinal virtues: prudence, justice, fortitude and temperance.

Our knowledge attains the stability of science only

through intellectual illumination. In like manner
our activity reaches the stable equilibrium of virtu-
ous acting only through the influence of divine action
which is the model and cause of all rectitude. Intellectual illumination takes place in the impression of the
idea of God on our intellect; moral illumination is
the gift of "synderesis" which, orientating our will
toward God, withdraws it from the mutability of its
impressions and affections and gives it the means
of grasping and imitating the most wise, most pure,
most strong and most just love of God. Through intellectual and moral illumination God bears man into
the very heart of being, and with man all the rest of
reality. Illumination places in man an indestructible
need for God because of which the intellect and will
turn to Him as to their proper perfection and the
source of their vigor; He is the cause and reason of
life. Through illumination man is naturally prepared
to know and love all things in God—to know and
love them as images and reflections of the divine
essence. The love and striving of man should be an
easy and joyous passage from God to things and
from things to God in perfect analogy to divine
knowledge and love. Thus, as he journeys onward
with facility and joy, man beholds Him, the traces
of Whom he finds in things and within Himself—
remembrances and traces of a beloved person. The
deep and full rationality of the universe and of each
thing should spring spontaneously from every object
which is encountered in experience. And each man
should find in his heart a new motive for inflaming
it with admiration and love of the supreme goodness
of God.

But why is reality so diverse? And why is it so difficult for man to know God, to see Him in things, to recognize and love His goodness in the thousand circumstances of life? Why, finally, in the human ascent to God, instead of facility and joy do we find arduous effort and suffering? The answer, of course, can only be one: because of original sin. St. Bonaventure, as every Platonic thinker, senses deeply the limitations and the misery of our actual condition, the contrast between that of which man is capable by his nature and that which is actually possible for him in his present state. This sentiment is common to every Christian thinker, but not all have developed it to the point of giving it a decisive position in philosophical thought. St. Bonaventure is of this latter group and places himself in a line of thought which stretches from antiquity to the present through St. Augustine and Pascal to Blondel.

Sin, entering into man, has certainly not destroyed his rational nature, his essential structure, but it has confused and obscured the idea and inclination impressed in his understanding and will, thus rendering their departure from God almost spontaneous; it has upset the natural order of his knowledge and his love. The world has ceased to be a book which speaks of the divine perfections, and the confusion of impressions and affections has taken away from the soul its security of decision and orientation. This explains how man can be deluded into seeking the bases of rationality and life within the boundaries of mundane reality. Having shattered the natural ladder which united him to God, man is left with a confused nostalgia and impotent desire for the infinite. Only with the help of grace can man succeed in laboriously reconstructing in himself that natural hierarchy of values which leads man to the objective reality of being.

The *Itinerarium mentis in Deum,* then, can only begin with a profound realization of one's own misery. Reflecting on its miserable state, the soul spontaneously emits a vital desire for its interior restoration and for prayer. "And since grace is the foundation of righteousness of the will, and of penetrating enlightenment of reason, we must first of all pray; next, we must live holily; then we must gaze at the spectacles of truth, and by gazing at them, rise step by step until we reach the mountain height where the God of gods is seen on Sion."[1] Since this Bonaventurian preface to philosophy sounds strange to our modern ears in its bare mediaeval formulation, it is necessary to acknowledge once again that the statement is still valid—that to know the truth one must love it and love it strongly. If we seek to distinguish the acts in which the love for truth is expressed, it will not be difficult to reduce them to two: control of the affections of passions and prayer, if not properly to Christ at least to substantial truth.

Grace purifies, enlightens and perfects. It purifies by sustaining good will in the attempt to re-establish clarity of vision and to gain the upper hand over the spiritual eye from all the deformations of a capri-confused tumult of the passions, thus freeing our

---

[1] "Sicut igitur gratia fundamentum est rectitudinis voluntatis et illustrationis perspicuae rationis; sic primo orandum est nobis, deinde sancte vivendum, tertio veritatis spectaculis intendum et intendendo gradatim ascendendum, quousque veniatur ad montem excelsum, ubi videatur Deus deorum in Sion." *Itinerarium,* c. I, n. 8; *Opera Omnia,* t. V, p. 298.

cious subjectivism. It enlightens indirectly by re-
moving the obstacles to the light which comes from
above, and directly by means of revelation. It perfects by bringing the likeness of man to God to the
highest degree possible in a creature. Only in this
way does man finally find himself in the ideal conditions necessary to begin his "itinerarium mentis"
toward God. Nothing can deceive him, nothing can
stop him. Freed from the encumbrances of sin and
the passions which deform the soul and confound its
"deformitas," his gaze and his affection pass from
things to God and from God to things almost with
the same facility and joy as that of man when he was
in the state of innocence. (We must keep in mind that
the model which St. Bonaventure has in mind for
this reunion with God and the life which he is con-
templating is that of St. Francis of Assisi.)

If this man turns to consider nature, he admires
the ordered and hierarchical variety of beings; the
beauty and grandeur of things; the order and vigor
in their acting; the constant harmony of the laws
which govern the movement of the heavens, and the
development of life. But his mind is never tempted by
that cosmic and pantheistic enthusiasm which is
known in every age; he sees the perfections of the
creature in their infinite source which is God and in
their ultimate reason which is His goodness. The
spontaneity, the beauty, and the sweetness of our
sensible relation with things through the pleasant
variety of sensations lift the mind to the eternal and
ineffable communication of the Three Divine Persons—the foundation and the law of all communication.

The contemplation of God becomes even more

immediate and profound if we reflect on our intellectual operations: the memory, understanding and will. Through the memory past things become present and we find in us immutable principles and concepts not abstracted from experience; with the understanding we define all things and demonstrate the necessary truth of many propositions; with the will we choose the best to which an inextinguishable desire carries us. Memory, then, which emancipates us in a certain sense from the vicissitudes of time, gives our soul a participation in eternity. The understanding, which by defining measures all things, confronting them with the idea of the most perfect being and with evident first principles, gives stability to our reasoning and, through this, a participation in eternal truth. The will, which pursues its good beyond every good which it encounters in this world, gives us proof that the supreme good is present and solicits its desire. Our intellectual operations reveal to us the great likeness of our soul to God. They are an experience in a certain real manner of the divine perfections in us. If we turn our consideration to the relations which exist among our three faculties, it will not be difficult to see how they are efficacious instruments for grasping the mystery of life and truth contained in the trinitarian dogma. Do not the sciences themselves, which are, as it were, intellectual habits of the soul, in their ternary divisions—natural, rational, moral; metaphysics, mathematics, physics; grammar, logic, rhetoric; individual, social and political morals—bring into relief the threefold rhythm of our soul and all reality?

Man could have arrived at this point by himself. Sin, however, has made necessary the restoration of grace, realized with the infusion of the three theological virtues which give to our soul the taste and sensibility for the supernatural, and with the teaching of Sacred Scripture which offers to our intelligence all of the doctrine of heavenly things. Here man learns the necessity, the laws, degrees, and stages of his return to God, disposed in a hierarchy of acts and disposition corresponding to the nine choirs of angels and the nine orders of the ecclesiastical hierarchy. The man who considers the marvelous order within himself, and endeavors to obey the impulses and suggestions which come to him from these reflections, spiritualizes the gaze of his mind, thus rendering it qualified for the highest meditations on God. There are in our soul ideas which transcend us—ideas which, fixed on it by a mind thus prepared, become rich sources of a manifold knowledge of God. We can contemplate God, St. Bonaventure teaches, not only in nature (*extra nos*) and its operations, and in the supernatural gifts of our soul (*intra nos*), but also "above us . . . through the light that shines upon our mind. This is the light of eternal truth."[2]

The reader who has followed us thus far will not find it difficult to identify this "lumen," which is in the soul but comes from God and lifts us above ourselves, with the idea of first or divine Being—the light of our intelligence in the sense explained. The deduction of the divine attributes has its proper

---

2 "Quoniam autem contingit contemplari Deum non solum extra nos et intra nos, verum etiam supra nos: extra per vestigium, intra per imaginem et supra per lumen, quod est signatum supra mentem nostram, quod est lumen Veritatis aeternae. . . ." *Itinerarium,* c. V, n. 1; *Opera Omnia,* t. V, p. 308.

source in this idea. We must observe at this point that, for St. Bonaventure, these progressive mental exercises leading to the knowledge of God are not cold philosophical speculations but loving contemplations, which, if they have the rigor of philosophical reasoning, also have the warmth of mystical contemplation. The truth is sought by the intellect, urged on, however, by the anxiety of a love which desires to know and then to embrace with intense fervor the truth known. Only under this condition does knowledge bring us nearer to God; only in this way does it become true progress in the soul's journey toward Him. A man may have the clearest ideas about God and still be far from Him. St. Bonaventure does not wish knowledge alone but also admiration and enthusiastic love. He desires, namely, an understanding in which the intellect and the will advance together, vying, as it were, with one another.

Besides being most Pure Being, God is also supreme or essential Goodness; because of this He is the supreme object of our will. If man were to take the time to attentively search the inner logic of pure goodness, he would advance a step further in the contemplation of God. The good is essentially "diffusivum sui." Considering the conditions of a perfect and infinite diffusion, he will quickly grasp the harmonious suitability of the trinitarian life which is precisely the most perfect realization of the logic of love. Certainly the human mind cannot entirely comprehend the marvels of this new mystery of the divine essence. Rather it would despair of being able, in the face of its impotence, to take the final step toward the contemplation of God if he were not assisted by the God-man. Christ gives hope and help to the soul through an even more perfect union with God. Encouraged by Christ Crucified, man increases the cries of prayer, enkindles his desire and calls for this supreme union through grace. The will reaches out for what the intellect cannot attain. It opens itself to the joy and intoxication of ecstasy, an ineffable state which cannot even be conceived by him who has not experienced it.

In ecstasy the soul does not achieve a more perfect conceptual knowledge of God, and for this reason the intellect remains, as it were, inoperative—an inactivity, however, which derives not from the absence of the object but from the inability of the intellect to grasp and hold it. It is an intellectual darkness which is caused by an excess, and not a lack, of light. It is an experience—and in this sense it is also knowledge—which escapes all our actual conceptual categories. Here the soul rests, for the will, which never ceases to be rational, leaps toward that mysterious presence in which it senses its Beloved sought through all its ways—the goal where all its desires and affections are filled with the serenity and security of him who has found all. The world vanishes with all its cares, desires, and fantasies. It is the most perfect anticipation of eternal glory.

III

The Importance of
The Thought of

saint Bonaventure

ITS ACTUAL AND DYNAMIC ASPECT

Mediaeval philosophy, which embraces the efforts —at times gigantic— of several generations of masters to elaborate a system of rational truth in harmony with revelation, was from the beginning prevalently Platonic. Among the varied and well-known reasons for this fact, the most important is certainly the authority and example of St. Augustine. Before the thirteenth century the influence of Aristotle had been confined to that of logic, in which he had been regarded as its principal source. In this century, however, it began to make itself felt in the field of metaphysics and, especially, physics. With St. Albert the Great and St. Thomas, the Aristotelian system was presented with two decisive interpretations and offered greater stability in comparison to that of Plato, which is always a little vague and fluctuating even on the most fundamental problems. After St. Thomas, the Augustinian School seems to give way to Aristotelianism and following another spurt of little importance, definitively withdraws from the field. Its reappearances in the following centuries never occur without leaving their mark and producing an atmosphere of heresy: Malebranche, Pascal, Rosmini, Laberthonnière and Blondel.

This is the historical view of Augustinianism

which is usually encountered in Catholic manuals on the history of philosophy. As a result, this current of philosophy has immense historical value but little or no theoretical value. Is this historical view of mediaeval philosophy just? And is such an evaluation of Augustinianism a true one? In these final pages I shall sincerely express my opinion regarding these questions, supporting it, of course, with suitable arguments.

The Augustinian School was not displaced from its position of privilege in the Church and the Schools of the thirteenth century without a struggle. The reaction to Aristotelian innovations soon began and it continued beyond the thirteenth century. Its means were the prohibitions of the Synods and the Pope, philosophical and authoritative arguments, and at times political maneuvers, like the attempt of William of Auvergne to profit from the strike at the University in 1229 by getting rid at one time of all the members of the faculty favoring Aristotle and substituting in their place Dominican and Franciscan masters loyal to Augustinianism. Historically, therefore, it is very true that we will never be able to clearly understand and give due importance to numerous pages of philosophers and theologians during these more than hundred years if we do not take account of this intellectual battle between the old Augustinian and new Aristotelian schools.

The earnestness with which the Augustinian masters participated in the struggle must be measured by the effort with which they strove to comprehend and assimilate as much as was possible the thought of Aristotle, rather than from the vehemence of certain episodes and certain polemic debates which are met with in their pages. It is very difficult to demonstrate from a historical point of view whether St. Thomas or St. Bonaventure or Duns Scotus was a more faithful interpreter of Aristotle. Up to this point there can be no disagreement among the students of mediaeval philosophy. But this is the obvious question: Is the struggle which the Augustinians waged against the Christian Aristotelianism of St. Thomas really based on theoretical causes and fundamental disagreements, or merely on misunderstandings? To put it differently, is it true that Thomism has left the substance of the Augustinian position out of its synthesis, or not? If the first hypothesis is true, then the hostility of the Augustinians has a serious foundation of theoretical interest (which is not directly concerned with its validity). If the second hypothesis is true, on the other hand, we must recognize that the conflict between the two schools was more a conflict of personalities than a conflict of ideas. In this case it is fortunate that it has settled down and it would be absolutely useless to stir it up again. It is precisely at this point that the students of mediaeval philosophy part ways.

Some of them, as Gilson for example, assert that Thomism makes no reply to the problems proper to Augustinianism. Even when the two schools seem to consider the same problem, each does so from its own point of view and with different preoccupations. Characteristic is the case of the problem of knowledge. While Thomistic Aristotelianism is satisfied to illustrate its psychological aspect, Augustinian Platonism disregards it in order to fix its attention on its metaphysical aspect. I have already spoken of this and will not elaborate further. Others, on the other hand, Monsignor Masnovo for example, are of the opinion that the Aristotelian method adopted by St. Thomas permitted him to go beyond the Augustinian School without sacrificing anything of its substantial views. The progress consists precisely in having simplified what was unduly complicated and having made more precise what was vague and poetic in the Augustinian position and solutions. In short, St. Thomas had made an advance beyond St. Augustine and his school analogous to that realized by Aristotle over Plato.

It is quite surprising that the evaluation of Bonaventurian thought proposed by the editors of Quaracchi fits in perfectly with this second line of thought. If, indeed, the differences between St. Bonaventure and St. Thomas are explained by the fact that the Seraphic Doctor did not have the chance to mine the treasure of Aristotelian thought, it is the same thing as saying—as I have already observed—that Augustinian philosophy finds its natural perfection in Aristotelianism. I cannot agree with this opinion.

First of all, the statement is at least rash that St. Bonaventure did not have a knowledge of Aristotle sufficient to take a position of dissent in regard to it with full knowledge of what he was doing. Furthermore, I cannot admit that the disciples of St. Bonaventure—intelligent and robust thinkers like Peckham, Matthew of Aquasparta and Roger Marston, to name only the most famous of them—fought the Aristotelian innovation with such ardor and tenacity only because of an equivocation; or because they were not aware that Thomism had saved substantially the Augustinian heritage. Although Duns Scotus may take an independent position, it is my conviction, based on long reflection on his most characteristic theses, that he should be placed in the Augustinian line which he also defends with all the power of his genius in the face of Aristotelian novelties. If the second hypothesis were true, it would be necessary to assert that the "subtle" Doctor had been taken in, or at least did not get to the bottom of things.

In the third place—and this succinct exposition of Bonaventurian thought has been an attempt to prove it—it seems to be absolutely necessary to admit more than an accidental and superficial difference between St. Thomas and St. Bonaventure. Certainly both are firm and united in the defense of the absolute transcendence of God in regard to creatures; thus they join forces against all the ancient and modern philosophical deviations which in some manner attack the divine transcendence. But in establishing and delineating the relationships which exist between the creature and the Creator, they follow different paths. The agreement on this fundamental metaphysical thesis does not prevent them from disagreeing on many other metaphysical, epistemological and psychological propositions. Nor is it any wonder! Reality presents such complex aspects that it is most difficult for the human mind to embrace them all. Precisely because no one is perfect, man will choose from among the various possible solutions the one which seems to him truer because more in harmony with his inclinations, his education, and the character of his genius. Only when the first principles enter directly into play—as in the problem of the transcendence of God—is the human mind constrained to bow before the overwhelming force of evidence.

In conclusion, I am convinced that the speculative

synthesis of St. Bonaventure, both as regards its methods and its results, is different from that of St. Thomas, even though not opposed to it. They present two views of reality which can be found to be complementary and contain the possibility of being integrated by a mind capable of uniting them in a higher synthesis. But this can be achieved, certainly, not through useless and cavilling polemics, but through honest study and calm reflection.

Having thus established the position of St. Bonaventure in comparison to that of the Angelic Doctor, it is necessary to clarify his relationship to St. Augustine. No one has ever doubted that philosophically St. Bonaventure is a disciple of St. Augustine; it is too evident. He is a disciple, however, who was in turn an original thinker. The thought of St. Augustine is encountered almost constantly in his works, but it is completely remolded into a new synthesis which often inserts modifications and adaptations, richer meanings and new logical connections into the doctrines which the Seraphic Doctor takes from his master. In assimilating the Augustinian theses, he does not merely repeat them but gives them new life while, nevertheless, always remaining faithful to the fundamental inspiration of the system. For this reason, notwithstanding its strongly original character, his speculation can be placed historically in the Platonic-Augustinian line.

He who recognizes not only historical but also theoretical value in the philosophical thought of a master, by this very fact defends its actual value for his own generation. Human problems are always living and always actual. He who has truly grasped them and has the intelligence to give them an original solution also has the right to be seriously consulted by him who in his turn takes up the task of re-thinking them; especially since some fruit is always gained from an encounter with great minds.

The Bonaventurian doctrines which I consider highly profitable to re-propose for the meditation of our contemporaries are three: St. Bonaventure's con-ception of man as the "imago Dei," his theory of in-tellectual illumination, and his critique of natural philosophy. Today we are all in need of defending ourselves against materialism and lifting ourselves beyond it; of making ourselves and others aware that the mind and heart of man are open to the infinite. In the Bonaventurian doctrine—which affirms God to be the proper object of our understanding and will, and hence places in relief our essential destina-tion in Him—we shall find motives, reflections and arguments for making known to all the right direc-tion of that desire for happiness which burns in the heart of every man. The resolving of the conflict be-tween empiricism and rationalism is in this way well on the way to being accomplished. To this end the Bonaventurian solution to the epistemological prob-lem, if it is clearly understood, seems to me capable of placing us on the right road to attain it—at least on a path more in tune with the modern ear.

That which St. Bonaventure attributes "a priori" to the human intellect is sufficient not only to satisfy rationalistic demands, but also to guarantee that acti-vity of the intellect in the face of sensible data, so dear to the heart of modern thought. On the other hand, this is not one of the usually dangerous conces-sions, since the doctrine of intellectual illumination has its foundation and reasons precisely in the limitations of man as a mutable and contingent creature. We likewise speak of the creativity of the human spirit. But we must keep in mind that this is a participated creativity which has its reality and its force in being an analogy, an imitation of the true creativity of the divine intellect. Another widely diffused error, which has become, one might say, the substance of modern thought and living, is naturalism, which, side by side with the creativity of the intellect, affirms the autonomy of human morals. The thought of St. Bonaventure is by its nature and from its inception a struggle against naturalism. To rethink and make known the severe Bonaventurian indictments against the enthusiasm of a philosophy autonomous and sufficient unto itself will be profitable for ourselves and others.

That these strictures are not out of place and, in fact, are susceptible of new development and conquest is not difficult to perceive today when the confusion in thought and action has become so vast, so clamorous, and so tragic. Following St. Bonaventure, we shall not arrive at the skeptical fideism typified by De Bonald and Lamennais. The Seraphic Doctor has not lost faith in human reason in itself— which he rather affirms capable by its nature of supreme truth—but of human reason buffeted and confused by the passions which man knows are so difficult to control without grace. To convince man of his actual misery is to cause him to take the first step toward his rehabilitation—available to all by the infinite mercy of God and made possible by the God-Man.

The doctrine of St. Bonaventure uniting thought with love is the perfect antithesis of that proud thinking to which we have been subjected by the exaggerated humanism of modern civilization. It is the true balance between exaggerated intellectualism and desperate irrationalism in which contemporary thought is embroiled.

The Notre Dame Pocket Library

A new paperback series, attractively produced, popularly priced.

PL-1   *Four Saints*. Louis Lavelle (translated by Dorothea O'Sullivan)   . $.95

PL-2   *Individuation. A Study of the Depth Psychology of Carl Gustav Jung*. Josef Goldbrunner (translated by Stanley Godman)   .   . $.95

PL-3   *The Problem of Population, Moral and Theological Considerations*. Donald N. Barrett, ed.   .   .   . $.95

PL-4   *Saint Bonaventure*. Efrem Bettoni (translated by Angelus Gambatese, O.F.M.)   .   .   .   .   . $.95

PL-5   *Holiness Is Wholeness*. Josef Goldbrunner   .   .   .   .   . $.95

PL-6   *The Problem of Population, Practical Catholic Applications*. Donald N. Barrett, ed.   .   . $.95

PL-7   *The Use of Parables in Catechetics*. Franz Mussner   .   .   . $.95

PL-8   *Christ and the End of the World. A Biblical Study in Eschatology*. Franz Mussner   .   .   .   . $.95

PL-9   *Cure of Mind, Cure of Soul: Depth Psychology and Pastoral Care*. Josef Goldbrunner   .   .   .   . $.95